The 401(k) Checkup

The Prescription for 401(k) Success

Richard E. Wilson II

The 401(k) Checkup

Printed by:
90-Minute Books
302 Martinique Drive
Winter Haven, FL 33884
www.90minutebooks.com

Published in the United States of America

160308-00366-2

ISBN-13: 978-0692698211
ISBN-10: 0692698213

For more information on 90-Minute Books including finding out how you can publish your own lead generating book, visit www.90minutebooks.com or call (863) 318-0464

Here's What's Inside...

Introduction

Everyone should have a chance to retire successfully. We all work hard for our money, but often the people who have the best shot at successful retirements are employees who have access to and save money in an employer-sponsored 401(k) plan. However, there can be a problem when plan sponsors are frequently too busy running their own companies, rather than their 401(k) plan.

This book has been written to share real world illustrations which I have encountered throughout the years. It is my goal to help you learn from what others have done and to be able to apply the lessons learned to your own circumstances. Naturally, we both want to see your employees, as well as yourself, enjoy a comfortable retirement. An example that comes to mind is when our team met with a management group from a manufacturing company. We reviewed their current plan, investment lineup, and vendor platform; as well as, the fees paid and the services provided. They were using one of the major 401(k) providers and had advisors who helped their investment committee do what appeared to be an excellent job at the company level.

However, a 401(k) is not supposed to be run for the benefit of the company. According to ERISA, a 401(k) plan must be run in the best interest of the participants.

Upon further examination, our team found that the participants were not able to access the advisor managing the plan without difficulty. In order to discuss anything with the advisor, they had to leave work at the end of a long shift and race to a town about an hour away.

We were able to offer a plan which proposed local group meetings, along with scheduled individual meetings before or after work as needed. We also offered online and/or phone conference meetings as requested. Furthermore, we could provide educational support via emails, social media, and printed copy throughout the year. Our goal was to help the workforce develop and achieve a successful savings plan, one that had been utilized by other companies similar to theirs with a large, blue-collar workforce making near-minimum wage. We also proposed a new vendor that would provide an open architecture fund selection. Our figures showed we could do all of this for 33% less than what they were currently paying in fees.

As you can see, my team and I want to help companies operate successful 401(k) plans that attract, retain, and motivate all employees. A plan which would take full advantage of tax deductions, maximize benefits, and align employees and corporate goals. This is all possible while still helping participants be retirement-ready when the time comes.

Hopefully, this book will educate you on the policies, procedures, and steps to be taken to operate a successful and compliant retirement plan and encourage you to have your own 401(k) checkup so you can determine the correct prescription for your 401(k) success.

To Your Success!

Richard E. Wilson II

Why Don't More ERISA Plan Sponsors Understand the Risk to Which They Are Exposed?

Since 2009, the Department of Labor (DOL) has been increasing its audits of 401(k) plans and continually increasing the number of auditors each year. According to the U.S. Department of Labor website, in 2015, it closed 2,441 civil investigations, with 1,640 of those cases resulting in monetary results for plans or other corrective actions. This amounts to about seven out of ten plans that were audited.

Of the audited plans, 275 criminal investigations were closed that resulted in 67 guilty pleas or convictions, and 61 individuals were indicted. Imagine going to the doctor for an annual checkup, being told that you have a disease and that seven out of ten people with your form of disease will be wiped out financially by dealing with the treatment. Of that 70%, 24% of them will die. To make it worse, your doctor could have known this ahead of time and recommended that you receive a vaccine regimen to help protect you against the disease in the first place.

This is exactly what I see happening in the 401(k) marketplace when plan sponsors rely on outside advisors that do not have the expertise and knowledge of the necessary processes. They think they are covered and acting prudently when, in reality, they may be exposing themselves to financial ruin and maybe even criminal charges.

About 16 years ago, I met the CFO (chief financial officer) of a local company with operations around the state and in northern California. The company had its 401(k) with one of the major investment houses. Fortunately, the CFO was open to meeting with me. My team and I shared how some new legislation made it possible to do some really exciting things using a plan design as well as offering a new investment strategy.

During our initial consultation, the CFO expressed a desire to be able to differentiate between the various groups and employees within the organization, but he knew that wasn't possible. As a Qualified Plan Financial Consultant (QPFC), I have worked within the 401(k) space for a significant number of years and am very knowledgeable about what can be accomplished. My team and I shared how we could treat the three different operating companies within their organization differently. We could break out the various levels of employees in those companies so that managers were treated differently than general employees. We could do something different for those in retail versus those in wholesale, and we could further break out senior management and owners.

"That's what I've been wanting to do!" the CFO burst out almost before we were through with our explanation.

We then shared how a fairly new investment strategy at that time called "Target Date Funds," was available through the platform we were recommending. These investments would allow the employees to invest their money in the appropriate mutual fund based on the date closest to when they would retire. The management of the fund would make appropriate changes over the course of time, taking into account market conditions. As an employee's date got closer, the management of the fund would get more and more conservative. This was a way to have a professional management team handle their money from early savings through retirement.

The CFO shared his excitement over this as well because most of the company's employees didn't know much, if anything, about investing, and many made just above minimum wage. The CFO thought our proposal would be a great way to help alleviate concerns the employees had and encourage their interest in participating in a plan.

It has been over 15 years since the company adopted this plan and the CFO still appreciates how well the plan works for his company, including additional services that have been included over time. For instance, online meetings were recently added which allows employees to access meetings from their own home using their computer or smartphone. As social media continues to evolve, we will continue to apply relevant methods to provide information at a time, place and method utilized by the participants.

Prudent Expert

Under ERISA, plan sponsors are required to be prudent experts with regard to 401(k)s and their operations, or they need to hire someone who is. To find out more visit the Department of Labor website at: www.dol.gov/ebsa/publications/fiduciaryresponsibility.html. This is a higher fiduciary standard than the more commonly used 'prudent man rule,' which is a typical fiduciary standard for non-ERISA fiduciaries. Plan sponsors also need to establish a prudent process, follow it, and document it.

While attending a 401(k) conference in Arizona in 2015, I attended a break-out session held by W. Andrew Larson, who is the Director of Retirement Education at Columbia Threadneedle Investments. He shared an important Supreme Court case involving Firestone®. The court had ruled that if the fiduciary followed their plan document, had a process and followed it, and then also documented it, the court would assume that the sponsor acted prudently.

Think about this another way: When you go to the doctor, he uses all kinds of specialized vocabulary. If someone working in the medical field didn't know these medical terms you probably would not consider them to be prudent experts. As a matter of fact, they probably wouldn't even have the job.

With this in mind, let's look at some of the "specialized words" connected with 401(k) plans.

Common 401(k) Terms

Some common terms are: 12(b)1, 404(c), auto enrollment, beneficiary, form 5500, fiduciary, and QDIA. What do all of these terms mean, and what do they relate to? I will assume that you are familiar with these. Now let's move on to some terms which are a little more difficult.

Terms that are a little more difficult include: ACP and ADP test, age-weighted allocation, alpha, beta, blackout period, cross testing, 3(16), 3(21), 3(38) fiduciaries, and HCE. Do you know all of these as well? Wow, you really know your stuff! Now let's move on to some of the most difficult ones.

These are really difficult terms: break in service, controlled group, EGTRRA, GIC, PPA, QACA, and Sub-TA fee. How confident are you feeling about your knowledge now? This specialized terminology is just scratching the surface. Please see the glossary of terms at the back of this book for more information on these and many other terms which was generously provided by Invesco.

"Reasonable Fees"

Plan sponsors also need to make sure that the fees being paid are reasonable. That doesn't necessarily mean they need to be the cheapest.

Reasonable fees can be illustrated by looking at the cost of a hammer. You might be able to get a hammer for $5. This is cheap, but if it breaks after you use it three or four times, it might not be such a good deal, especially if you are a contractor using your hammer every day. You would be better off paying $50 for a hammer that will last your entire career. This would be considered reasonable or a good value for the money you spent.

Thus the question, when it comes to 401(k) plans: Are you and your employees getting additional services, or value, for the money you are paying? Keep in mind that "cheap" implies poor quality, while "inexpensive" represents a good value. Would you overpay your suppliers or employees by 10%, 20%, 30%, or more? If you wouldn't personally do that, then why would you act in the same way with your employees' money, for which you have a very high fiduciary level of obligation?

Let's consider this "reasonable fees" discussion in conjunction with the CFO illustration at the beginning of this book. That particular CFO was a self-proclaimed cheapskate. He would proudly tell you how much money he could save. So, do you think the plan design and services we offered was the cheapest plan? Would it work for him? Needless to say, we were not the cheapest; we may have even been a bit more expensive than average. However, our design features required additional work and testing to make sure that we stayed in compliance with the government's version of "fair" (which is also referred to as testing).

We also had a platform that offered significantly more services to the participants, as well as to the plan sponsor. For the first time, the plan trustees were going to be able to see how their employees utilized the resources offered. There would be multi-city tours each year to bring education to the employees. The employees also had the ability to call the advisor directly to discuss concerns personally. The trustees would be able to see how many people called the 800-number, or logged into the website, and what the results were.

We added social media as a means of delivering educational content to the employees. Also, by using LinkedIn and Facebook, we were meeting the participants where they were. This allowed them to access a personal advisor whenever and however they needed.

Information that could now be gathered could then be used to help determine future education which would address concerns or topics that were of interest to the employees. Comprehensive reports would show how many participants were invested in only one fund and what type of fund that was. Cash balance increases would become evident during times of market volatility and we could provide emails or set up meetings to talk about what was currently happening. All this information would be documented and archived for future reference.

The CFO soon recognized that he was getting good value for the money his company was spending. The lower cost offerings were indeed "cheaper," but they were not really "better."

I further surprised this CFO the first time I proposed a reduction in the fee calculation I used for my services. You see, as the plan grew, and the work I did leveled off, I didn't need to charge the same rate so I passed this saving on to the company and its employees. This has happened three times so far over the years.

Qualifications

It is not uncommon for many advisors serving 401(k) plan sponsors today to **not** obtain the proper education or credentials; or maintain their credentials or participate in ongoing annual trainings. Like many general-practice doctors, they have what appear to be the skills to serve their clients, but since they do not specialize in this specific field, they may not recognize a disease—breaches—and thereby expose their patients to unnecessary risk. By neglecting the specialized education or conferences specific to 401(k) plans they may not be staying on top of industry trends and issues. They may also be unaware of new legislative requirements, and these advisors could be unfamiliar with how to grow 401(k) plans or how to help their clients obtain benefits through the offering of a plan. Every plan sponsor should be evaluating their service partners with this in mind.

You might be wondering what kind of credentials you should be looking for. One credential could include the QPFC (Qualified Plan Financial Consultant) from the *American Society of Pension Professionals and Actuaries.* Another is QKA (Qualified Plan Administrator) from the same organization. Maybe they have the CKP from the *Retirement Advisor University.*

Other questions to consider are: How long have these advisors served in this specific marketplace? What is their well-designed process, and how will it help the plan sponsors as fiduciaries, as well as protect the plan? All of these credentials require an extensive knowledge of things specific to 401(k)s and other corporate sponsored retirement plans along with the examinations, depth of experience and continuing education.

I reached out to a bank that offered a 401(k) to its employees because I had noticed some items of concern from their 5500 filings, which are a matter of public record. I met with the head of human resources and found out that everyone had their own individual accounts and were purchasing A-share mutual funds at full load. This load is a large, upfront cost for retail investors; it generally ranges from 4% to 5.75 %, most of which is paid to the advisor.

I consulted with the bank on what they wanted to accomplish and about how to incorporate a plan design which would also help facilitate the employers' desire to engage the employees in supporting the company's corporate goals. I assembled a professional team of service providers to support me in this. ING was to be the vendor providing the platform. A third-party administrator (TPA) would provide additional services including preparation of plan amendments, summary plan descriptions, etc. I would then coordinate with both of these service providers to follow the identified processes and procedures needed to operate a compliant 401(k) plan and do it for a competitive price. I would also organize group meetings in multiple cities and make it possible for the participants to meet with me individually.

Educational materials and training would be provided to help the employees make decisions that were in their best interest, as well as helping them document it for their own records. This could all be done for a fee of about one half of one percent. The TPA and ING were to be paid according to their schedules, and all together we were at a cost lower than what they were presently paying.

This amazing cost savings included the fact that more service would be provided for a fraction of what the existing advisor charged. The bank loved the proposal so much they took the vendor, processes, procedures, and scheduled items then asked their existing advisor to implement them. Unbeknownst to me, the advisor on the plan was a high school buddy of the president of the bank.

Do you think this company acted prudently? Do you think it did what was in the best interest of the participants? If the Department of Labor (DOL) were to audit this plan, how would they view it?

Department of Labor (DOL) & Internal Revenue Service (IRS)

Plan sponsors also need to keep in mind that there are two government agencies involved in the oversight and auditing of 401(k) plans: the DOL and the IRS (Only the government would determine that two different organizations should be involved...). Like many entities, these two organizations sometimes have challenges working well with each other. Unfortunately, it's the plan sponsors who often can be caught in the middle.

Here's what each department covers, according to the IRS website: The IRS has primary jurisdiction over the qualified status of 401(k) plans, which includes examining plans and processing requests for determination letters. The DOL has primary jurisdiction over the fiduciary standards, reporting, disclosure requirements and other rules that do not affect the qualified status of 401(k) plans.

The importance of this was made very clear while I was attending a 401(k) conference in San Diego this year. W. Andrew Larson explained how the IRS had been pretty active in their oversight of 401(k) plans right from the beginning. Service providers quickly adapted to the rules they developed and today we have things like Top Heavy, ACP and ADP testing to stay in ready compliance. (see glossary of terms for more information on these and other terms)

However recently, the U.S. Department of Labor published a new rule in April 2016 related to qualified retirement accounts. The rule introduces an additional fiduciary standard under the Department of Labor that will start to take effect in 2017 and be fully effective by 2018. A fiduciary standard means that advisors must put client's interests ahead of their own and recommend products that are in the client's best interest. This rule applies to financial services firms and advisors across the industry when making recommendations for qualified retirement accounts such as IRAs.

I consult with my clients on how to make sure they stay in compliance with the laws. I also take that opportunity to work with them on how to integrate their corporate goals into the design and operation of their 401(k) plans.

Recently, I met with a security company that wanted to start a 401(k) plan. They recognized the need of this benefit to attract quality employees but were unsure if the cost was worthwhile.

Finding out more about their business and what they felt they needed to accomplish to be successful was an essential step. It became evident that they didn't want employees taking unnecessary risks which would result in injury, thereby affecting their workers' compensation cost and causing overtime for others while the injured employee recuperated.

The company also wanted to add new clients, especially within the neighborhoods where they already had security patrols since it could result in additional revenue without the cost of additional patrols. They also needed to retain their employees and were concerned that the coming increases in the minimum wage over the next six years could cause their pay packages to be less competitive than it would be for their employees to flip burgers. Finally, the owners wanted to be able to resume saving for their retirement, as they had been digging into their own retirement funds to get the company up and running.

Based on this, I suggested that every year they determine what their business goals were. Goals that, if achieved, would help them be in a position to share a contribution with the employees through profit-sharing. The employees would be vested over a six-year period, so that if they left their jobs before that, they would only get a portion of these funds, or the vested amount. Over time these funds would grow which could provide an incentive to remain with the company. Additionally, the company would help the employees feel like they were important to the success of the business while giving them a reason to encourage their co-workers to stay with the company in order to also receive those profit-sharing contributions.

Our team also recommended that they set up the plan so that everyone was automatically enrolled as soon as they were eligible. This way, the owners knew that they were doing everything they could to help the employees be retirement-ready when the time came. This would also help create a higher contribution level which is needed for the owners to be able to start saving large sums. The owners need to be able to contribute and not have problems with the testing that the government requires to ensure that the plan is fair to everyone. Such a fairness measurement is conducted through top-heavy, ADP and ACP testing and has nothing to do with actually being fair. Actually how does one define fair and to whom? One analysis might be to show that a smaller contribution to a younger employee and a larger contribution to an older employee might, over time, create an equivalent value at their respective retirement ages. Another thought might be that everyone gets the same amount regardless. Both of these could be argued as both fair or unfair depending on your point of view.

With this in mind, I further recommended that we create three groups of employees: the owners, the managers, and the security officers. Each group would be rewarded differently under the profit-sharing plan. For instance, the owners would get the largest portion, while the managers would receive a slightly higher percentage than the security officers. Since this contribution was not part of their payroll, the payroll taxes would not be assessed, allowing more money to go to the participants for the same cost to the employer. We also discussed using a non-elective safe harbor match which is a profit sharing contribution that is immediately vested as a means of encouraging the employees to save and to help them buy out of the other tests that are often used to determine fairness. Imagine how this business owner felt having just been shown a way to get his employees to think and act like owners striving to help each other, while increasing profitability. We had come up with a way to help regain his lost retirement savings that had been used in the start-up of the business. It could also help reduce employee turnover and alleviate his concerns over competitive compensation as the minimum wage increases came along in the coming years.

As part of the plan, I would work with the owner to develop an investment policy statement that outlined how he would evaluate vendors and funds to determine which were appropriate, and how they should be offered to employees. Together, we would measure those investments against the criteria we used in the investment policy statement. We would also establish a minimum number of criteria, (generally six to seven) out of the 12 possible measures, and create a written report with easy-to-understand breakdowns and graphics. This printed report would become part of the fiduciary record, documenting what was reviewed, what was decided, and what was actually done.

Every few years we would conduct an in-depth analysis of the vendor and the price they charged to maintain the plan. Again, we would have a written report documenting the various fees, including those of the individual funds based on the amounts invested in those funds. These results would be displayed visually using a bar graph showing the growth of the funds over various time periods. We would additionally have a chart clearly delineating various amounts from the existing vendor, as well as the ones against which they were benchmarked. Again, this written record would become part of the permanent fiduciary record file.

When we look to the courts and the Firestone® case we find that this well-established process, when followed and documented, can "vaccinate" or help protect a plan's sponsor in the event of an audit, while showing that prudence and the best interests of the participants are being adhered to. All the while this documented process is conducted using tools that are independent of the vendors offering services in order to help ensure impartiality.

Don't Focus on Results; Focus on Process

By now you must realize I take pride in working with my clients in helping them achieve success. My role is to manage and help mitigate risk by utilizing a consultative approach on behalf of the financial safety of your organization, specifically as it relates to the operation of the 401(k). This helps free up your time, so you can focus on the priorities of running and growing your business while knowing that your employees are being taken care of and are receiving tools and resources to help them get on track towards achieving their retirement goals.

As a Qualified Plan Financial Consultant with years of experience in the 401(k) field, I am able to guide you through a successful, proven, and documented process to meet your obligations, as well as providing education and insight to your employees. I will help you utilize a variety of tools to help you stay in compliance. Together, we will work to educate your employees using printed materials, email, LinkedIn and Facebook.

401(k) Online Presence & Tools

Have you ever Googled your company's retirement plan? One of the top listings will be from BrightScope®.

BrightScope® provides free ratings and rankings for 401(k) plans and advisors. If you have fewer than 100 employees, BrightScope® will probably not have enough information to rate your plan at this time. However, if you have over 100 employees, then your plan is most likely required to complete an annual audit, a copy of which is available through the Department of Labor's website as public information.

BrightScope® uses the information it gathers from these public records to rate plans. Since this rating is only garnered from public documents, it doesn't really represent a true rating. Also, BrightScope® doesn't always take into account the plan size, services provided, or the process that the plan sponsor may be using to operate the plan in the best interest of the participants. It analyzes only the fees and compares them to those of other companies that it feels are in the same industry.

The same website also provides information about advisors, but there are downsides. If the advisor is not allowed by his company to contribute posts or answer questions on their interpretation of the laws in an online, undocumented process, the advisor might not be ranked very high. The advisor's broker dealer also might not permit endorsements or recommendations of the advisor in online venues. Various firms view these requirements differently, so some advisors may have posts of recommendations, or the advisor's company may be unaware that it is being done in violation of their company policy. Regardless, this website provides background and other information that is valuable to a plan sponsor. The IRS also provides another great resource you should use as a plan sponsor, that allows you to self-check your plan. They have a 401(k) plan checklist with questions that you can easily complete which is located at www.IRS.gov/pub/irs-pdf/p4531.pdf.

Make note of which items you are taking care of as plan sponsor and which items are taken care of by your advisor, third-party administrator and vendor. A plan sponsor should sit down with their chosen advisor and review their process to see what they need to do to stay in compliance. They need to ask themselves, “Does this process make sense? Can I comply? Is it documentable? Is there an independent tool that confirms results while remaining impartial?” I like to use the tools and reports from the *Center for Fiduciary Management*, as it provides independent tested results.

After this, the plan vendor platform needs to be evaluated. Are the services that are desired the ones being offered? How is the usage of those services being communicated to the sponsor and documented for the process? Are the participants being provided the information and education needed to make informed choices? What methods of delivery—like social media and email—are being used to ensure that employees are constantly receiving important information? When an extraordinary event or circumstance occurs, is this conveyed to the plan sponsor and the employees?

Then, working with the advisor, the plan sponsor should develop an annual calendar of what will be done, by whom, and when. This includes reviews, online meetings, internet webinars, trainings, etc. Each year the annual review needs to be completed, documented, and archived. Every three to five years a comprehensive fee and services benchmarking needs to take place. This process needs to be repeated for the life of the plan.

By taking all of these steps, you are, in essence, "vaccinating" yourself against a future audit by creating a documented, written record. In the event of an audit you will be able to readily furnish the items needed and or requested by the auditor showing your adherence to the ERISA requirements. Keep in mind that the government doesn't expect you to know the future; it does expect you to be taking a diligent approach to looking out for the best interests of your employees.

The Prescription for a Successful 401(k)

In order to have a successful 401(k), plan sponsors need to know why they are even offering one. If they want employees who are motivated and engaged, ones who want to help grow the business and ideally be able to successfully retire with a lifestyle they want, then offering this type of plan can be ideal.

Providing a 401(k) allows a business to stay competitive. It helps to attract and retain quality employees. It allows for the owner, as well as the employees, to save for their future on a tax-preferential basis. It provides the means for a business to engage their employees in the success of the business and allows the business to share the profits without payroll taxes in a manner that rewards the employees and encourages them to stay while potentially allowing the owner to retain the greater portion of this allocation. It can allow for owners and other highly compensated employees to save for retirement—at a much higher level—when they otherwise might be unable to do so due to taxation phase-outs. It can even provide a means to save in a Roth IRA account that they would not be able to take advantage of outside of the 401(k).

Saving into the retirement plan may also allow employees to take advantage of federal tax credits through the Savers Tax Credit. See the IRS published chart for 2016 below.

2016 Saver's Credit			
Credit Rate	Married Filing Jointly	Head of Household	All Other Filers*
50% of your contribution	AGI not more than $37,000	AGI not more than $27,750	AGI not more than $18,500
20% of your contribution	$37,001 - $40,000	$27,751 - $30,000	$18,501 - $20,000
10% of your contribution	$40,001 - $61,500	$30,001 - $46,125	$20,001 - $30,750
0% of your contribution	more than $61,500	more than $46,125	more than $30,750

Source: irs.gov

Money saved also allows all participants to pool their funds to gain better pricing on investment choices and money saved within a 401(k) is generally protected from bankruptcy proceedings. For a doctor, lawyer, or other professional who may be at a greater risk of lawsuits, this can be invaluable. A 401(k) can also be used in combination with cash balance plans to supercharge the savings rate and reduce the overall current tax liability for high-wage-earning professionals, especially self-employed individuals.

Supercharged 401(k)

If your company is looking to supercharge retirement savings and has the necessary cash flow to support this then adding a cash balance plan may allow you to do just that. According to Kravitz Inc., a recognized leader in the cash balance plans with over 1200 plans nationwide, the 2016 Maximum Contribution Limits for 401(k), Profit Sharing & Cash Balance Plans looks like this.

Age	401(k) only	401(k) with Profit Sharing	Cash Balance	TOTAL
60-65	$24,000	$59,000	$249,000	$308,000
55-59	$24,000	$59,000	$201,000	$260,000
50-54	$24,000	$59,000	$153,000	$212,000
45-49	$18,000	$53,000	$117,000	$170,000
40-44	$18,000	$53,000	$90,000	$143,000
35-39	$18,000	$53,000	$68,000	$121,000
30-34	$18,000	$53,000	$52,000	$105,000

Source: Kravitz Ideal Candidates for Cash Balance Plans

This information is general in nature and is not a substitute for legal advice in a particular case.

Your 401(k) plan design can and should support corporate goals. When a business decides to incorporate its business goals with a 401(k), the benefits to the organization can be significant.

First, the business needs to ensure that it is engaged in the best practice of creating goals and a business plan for the year. These goals identify what needs to be done to achieve certain company objectives. By sharing these goals with employees, everyone gets engaged in achieving them, so they can share in the success of the business. It is through this intelligent design that everyone is rewarded according to their role within the company. This allows the owners, managers, and employees to be rewarded differently, thereby, allowing the owners to receive the highest percentage, management to receive the second highest percentage, and employees the third. These groups can be broken up into whatever business model makes sense, as long as the discrimination decided upon is based on permitted criteria. Determining the model based on hair color or gender, for instance, would not be permitted.

In a doctor's office the model could be doctors, administrative staff, nurses, lab personnel, etc. Tying this sharing in the success of the business to corporate goals helps eliminate the entitlement attitude that I generally see developing after three years of making contributions to a 401(k) when it is not tied to specific goals. The employees come to expect that they are going to get the profit-sharing contribution and when they don't, they become disgruntled. This is not a good thing.

The use of a vesting schedule over six years helps keep the employees around to become fully vested and thereby retain 100% of the profit sharing and the associated investment returns. By incorporating auto enrollment and escalation to the plan, it can help your employees stay on track for a successful retirement. You are also clearly demonstrating that you are operating the plan in the best interest of the participants as required under ERISA. This can be combined with a stretch match which involves some type of tiered structure, such as dollar for dollar on the first 3% and fifty cents to the dollar on the next 4%, to get the full match. This will generally encourage employees to stick with a higher savings plan to help them be retirement-ready when the time comes.

Helping employees successfully retire is likely one of the most important benefits to the company. How does this support the company? First, it is most likely a means to attract and retain the kind of quality employees that really help the business succeed. The employees are more likely to be content and look forward to the future with either reduced, or no financial concerns. They know that they are on track to a more confident retirement. They will work to help the company meet its goals and most likely exceed the success targets set by the owners or management. They will be able to advance within the company because older workers will eventually retire when the time comes. Imagine the benefits of low turnover and highly motivated employees who actively try to assist the company with its goals.

Fees

When designing plans, consider how the fees will be paid? Are they going to be billed directly to the company? Will they be taken from employees' accounts based on their account value (which is the most common option)? Will it be some combination of both of these options?

A 401(k) is an employee benefit, so any charges paid by the employer are deductible to the employer unless those fees are paid from plan assets. This is often predominantly done by the business owner and other key employees because they have the bulk of the money invested within the plan. You, the owner, are likely paying the bulk of the fees to operate your plan and yet you get no tax deduction for it, which reduces your account value.

Instead, you could change this by having some of the cost allocated on a per-person basis. This way, everyone pays their portion of plan costs. Alternatively, you could also decide to pay the plan costs at the company level and get a tax deduction for it.

ERISA is the governing body of law which a plan sponsor needs to be aware of. It has many intricacies that require a sponsor to perform in helping to ensure compliance. Perhaps because of these intricacies, within the legal field itself there are fewer attorneys who specialize in the laws relating to ERISA and retirement accounts.

Healthy Action Items

Doctors meet with their patients annually to assess how they are doing. They generally make recommendations such as, "Get more exercise, lose some weight, take medications to help ward off serious future ailments." This is all for the health or best interests of their patients.

ERISA requires the same thing. First, the plan must be operated in the best interests of the participant. This means that you should review your plan documents every year. You should also have an established process that handles the 'who, what, when, where, why, and how.' Confirm that you are following your documents and that they are up-to-date with the most recent amendments required by the DOL. Receive, review, and understand the 408(b)2 and 405(a) fee disclosure documents provided by your vendor. Utilize tools and resources to evaluate whether the fees being paid are reasonable. Remember, the point isn't for the plan to be the cheapest. The plan fees should be reasonable enough that your employees are receiving a good value for the amount paid. Review the investment choices for compliance with the investment policy statement and remember that performance is not the standard by which to measure.

The DOL doesn't expect you to have a crystal ball and know what the future of the stock market is. It wants to see that you are using reasonable standards to measure how an investment is performing given the market's condition and in relation to its peers. Place funds on a watch list when necessary, and document why they are there. Lastly, you should replace funds when they are no longer appropriate.

Another critical factor is to provide the necessary services, tools, and education to help employees make informed decisions. Just having a website where employees can look at a prospectus and review performance and holdings does not provide enough information for them to make informed decisions. This is especially true if the employees don't understand what a mutual fund is in the first place. Encourage participants to take advantage of advisors who provide the service to the plan for group education, webinars, phone conferences, and in-person meetings. If you don't have an advisor who can assist the employees in this manner, hire one. This can be accomplished in many ways, including a consultation, or on a contract basis. Develop a calendar that clearly communicates how and when these services are available, and make sure that required notices and communications are provided to participants in a timely fashion.

Lastly, conduct an independent evaluation of your vendor and the fees being paid by seeking bids from other providers every three to five years. This kind of benchmarking helps ensure that fees being paid for services rendered are still reasonable given the plan's current demographics and value. Keep in mind that this is just a summary of what needs to be done and is not meant to be a comprehensive list of all activities required under ERISA.

You may be thinking that you are doing everything you need to be doing, but there are still things you should consider. For instance, when was the last time you checked the value of assets in the plan and made sure that the plan's fidelity bond was adequate? This is one of the easiest red flags that I have seen as it is reported on the IRS Form 5500 filed each year. A simple criterion like this could be the source of a simple computer algorithm that the DOL or an attorney looking for targets could run.

Another thing to consider is whether you have an investment policy statement. ERISA doesn't require it, but if you receive a notice of audit by the Department of Labor, it will be one of the documents they ask for. If they ask for it, don't you think it's important enough to have one?

How many investment selections do you make available for your employees to invest in? You might think you need a large number to fully cover all potential investment ideas. You could be wrong, because after about 24 choices, participants tend to become overwhelmed and have an even harder time making choices about how to invest. They can easily become frozen with indecision.

Another thing to consider is only having auto-enrollment and escalation for the new employees. That unintentionally leaves out the employees already in the plan. Or maybe you don't even have auto enrollment and escalation.

If you knew that your employees would not be able to retire when they reached retirement age, would you do something about it? Do you think this would meet the standard for operating the plan in the best interest of the participants?

While attending a 401(k) conference, I was fortunate enough to hear a great explanation from Charlie Epstein, The 401k Coach®, using this illustration he said Imagine you are at the airport, waiting to board your plane, and this announcement comes over the loudspeakers: Attention, folks! Boarding is about to begin, and we just wanted to inform you that there is an 85% chance that we will not arrive at our desired destination and/or be on time. Thank you for choosing to fly with us." Not saving at all or not saving enough for retirement, is the same as getting on that plane!

You need to review how the services offered are being utilized. If you provide doctor visits that are pre-paid, but no one is going to see the doctor, that is a potential problem. Maybe employees don't know that they can see the doctor, or maybe they don't want to see the doctor and would rather not have that service. What about that website and 800-number that you provided for participants to access their accounts and information? If nobody goes online or calls the 800-number, there could be a need that is not being met.

Another commonly overlooked consideration is lots of money in cash money market or stable value investments. A 401(k) is a retirement account; unless retirement is less than 18 months away, participants should generally not have large balances in these 'near to cash' investments. This generally happens because of market volatility and fear of loss, as most people make investment decisions based on how they feel and not the well-thought-out decisions based on knowledge and experience.

I like to ask the following question at nearly all of my meetings to help employees understand what they are doing: “What feels better, making money in the stock market or losing money in the stock market?”

Everyone responds, “Making money.” However this is generally wrong! Losing money in the market is what actually feels good. At this point they generally think “What is this guy talking about?”

I go on to explain that when the markets are doing well, employees often will finally decide to start investing their money and those investments can often be into riskier investments because of their high recent returns, which are appealing. When the market starts going down, they start to worry. If the market keeps going down, they start losing sleep. Then the market goes down a bit more, and in exasperation, they throw up their hands, sell their investments, and go back to cash. I often hear them say, “Thank goodness, I got out!” That’s the feel-good part.

Then the market starts going up, and up, and up some more. Finally, they decide to get back into the market, thinking that this time is different. When the market starts going down, down, down, they panic and they sell again. This process is often repeated until they have no money, but it felt good along the way. At least, some of the time it did.

The reverse of that is easy to see when you look back at the recent Great Recession of December 2007 until June 2009. Everyone knew at least one friend or family member who lost their job and/or their home. The economy was in the toilet with no end in sight. That was the time to buy. Do you remember how that felt?

Imagine attending a 401(k) meeting back then where I told you that now is likely a once-in-a-lifetime opportunity to invest. If you have any extra money or savings, this is a good time. Many of those employees probably wondered if I was crazy.

At that time the Dow Jones Industrial Average was around 6,600 and proceeded to advance to 18,000 over the next six years. That is almost triple what it was back then. It took a lot of courage to invest at this time and I can assure you that virtually no one felt good about making investments during this time of chaos, but those who did likely saw significant growth.

Most employees don't have the desire, or the knowledge, to determine when to get in and out of the market and they definitely don't want to spend the time monitoring it. When you look at the returns of the S&P 500® Index, simply missing the ten best days over the last 20 years reduced your return by almost 50%.

Getting into and out of the market is for traders not investors. It also represents a higher level of risk than someone should probably be taking over the long-haul towards and being in retirement. That is why having an investment plan that keeps employees invested all the time, and at an appropriate risk level as they get closer and closer to retirement, is so important.

Another common pitfall is not allowing for early rollover within the plan. This is also known as the in-service distribution. Not allowing this feature may cause the employees to worry excessively since they may not be able to afford to take a 20% to 50% hit to their account balances. This level of loss may be the difference between retiring and not being able to retire as planned or at the very least, significantly impact the lifestyle during retirement. Many may want to seek out other investments that aren't available within the plan.

One of the worst pitfalls that a plan sponsor can fall into is doing a review and then being shown by a different advisor that working through the same, or a different vendor, could result in significant cost savings to employees and then not taking advantage of that. When conducting plan benchmarking for a potential client, I often show them that they can save about 30% and receive the same or more services for themselves and their employees. Often, they "like" their current advisor and don't feel comfortable changing to a specialist, or they don't want to deal with the hassle of making a change. What they fail to see is that they aren't handling their own money; it's the employees' money.

Would you overpay one of your suppliers or employees by 30%? If you wouldn't do that with your own money, why would you do it with your employees' money? Keep in mind that failure to follow the fiduciary rules exposes plan sponsors to personal liability, and I think we can all agree that overpaying by 30% would not be considered "reasonable" which is required under ERISA. In fact, failure to follow the fiduciary rules can expose plan sponsors to personal liability.

I was once in the process of becoming advisor to a 401(k) plan, which involved having a meeting with an owner and his committee. We were discussing how and where the money was invested in order to get more details about their irregular investments. The committee shared that a large portion of the funds were invested in non-traditional loans that were secured by real estate. What made them non-traditional was that they were loans made to the customers of the company. When one of the company's customers needed a loan, and money wasn't presently available but would be soon—based on another loan payoff—the owner would just put his own money into the plan so the loan could be made. When the payoff came, he would take his money back out. His logic was that these loans helped ensure that the employees had jobs and that he was just cash-flowing the process when he put extra money in and later withdrew it.

My team and I decided not to take on this plan due to our concerns about ERISA violations; as well as, our concerns over the fighting that was taking place within the committee over which of them would receive which loan as we worked to get their plan into compliance.

About two years later, I heard back from one of my contacts at this company. They had been audited. It took over a year, and they had to hire U-Haul trucks to transport all of the documentation that was requested. The response letter at the close of the audit had so many pages it was over an inch thick.

Another common pitfall is not doing anything. I recently met with two different plan sponsors. One was a pharmacy, and the other was a large, multi-company organization that did both private and government operations.

The pharmacy's advisor left the company and moved to another state to be with his new bride. Six months later, the company had not replaced the advisor. This was a very big deal.

First, the company had a plan that paid an advisor to provide support to the organization and employees. If there was no advisor doing this, they were paying for something that was not being done. When I stopped by the pharmacist's office last week, I asked her if she would order drugs from one of her suppliers, pay for the drugs, and then allow that supplier to not deliver the drugs. She responded with an emphatic "No." Yet, that was in essence what she was doing with the 401(k) plan.

The company with both private and public sector work also had an advisor who left. Their plan paid for an advisor who in addition to providing services to the plan and its participants would meet with a number of employees who were retiring every year. With no advisor, this didn't happen. Furthermore, they conducted their annual plan review in December, and their advisor left a couple of months prior to that.

Both companies above are breaching their fiduciary duties and placing themselves and their personal assets at risk.

When doing a vendor comparison, or benchmarking, it is imperative that you have a way to compare them that prudently matches fees being charged. This is one of the most difficult things to do because there are so many different sources of revenue for the providers. There are different share classes that charge different fees; there are 12(b)1 fees, sub-TA fees, asset based fees, direct bill fees, and per participant fees.

To really understand all this, you need an advisor who can help you standardize all of these fees, project what the total cost is, and convey that to you in an easy-to-understand format. One way to do that is a bar graph that shows the results of fees on the growth of assets over time. (For an example for illustrative purposes only, see Figure 1 Next Page)

Composite Returns	YTD	1 YR	3 YRS	5 YRS	Net Exp.	Wrap Fee Exp. Ratio	Total Exp. (Net plus Wrap)
Existing John Hancock Lineup	0.25	-2.22	4.40	4.65	0.66	-0.32	0.33
Paychex Proposal	1.03	-0.90	5.38	5.66	0.18	0.00	0.18
Principal Proposal	1.25	0.33	5.45	5.78	0.15	0.00	0.15
Nationwide Proposal	0.91	-0.14	5.89	6.30	0.40	0.00	0.40

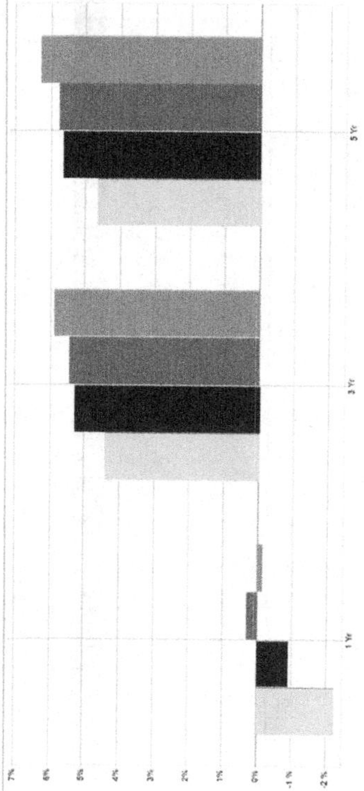

The Plan Composite Return is presented net of fees.

Performance data shown represents past performance. Past performance does not guarantee future results. Investment return and principal value of an investment in fund(s) will fluctuate so that an investor's shares when redeemed may be worth more or less than their original cost. Composite performance data shown is calculated net of fees and reflects any reinvestment of dividends and other distributions and the deduction of fees and expenses.

Source: www.firmcmx.fiduciarymanagement.com

It is also useful to have a spreadsheet that clearly shows the annual total cost of various fees with a total line at the bottom that displays the current vendor all-in cost against those that were part of the benchmarking process. (See Figure 2 on the next page)

Fee Description	Existing John Hancock Lineup		Paychex Proposal		Principal Proposal		Nationwide Proposal	
	Units	Fees	Units	Fees	Units	Fees	Units	Fees
Weighted Net Expense (BPS)	66	$30,068	18	$8,240	15	$7,012	40	$18,378
Wrap Fees (BPS)	-32	($14,818)	0	$0	0	$0	0	$0
Administration/Recordkeeping Fee (BPS)	35	$16,010	24	$10,978	35	$16,010	35	$16,010
Record Keeper (BPS)	48	$21,957		$0	21	$9,606	40	$18,297
Advisor Fees (BPS)		$0	44	$20,127	38	$17,382	38	$17,382
Total Fees		$53,217		$39,345		$50,010		$70,068
Total Expense Ratio		1.16%		0.86%		1.09%		1.53%

Notes	
Existing John Hancock Lineup	fee info is based on john hancock annual review report info provided by craig
Principal Proposal	Please see official proposal from Vendor to confirm pricing. The information here is believed to be accurate but will not replace actual proposal.
Nationwide Proposal	admin/recordkeeping fee is same as listed for the existing provider record keeper fee is Nationwides charge per proposal
	these fees are believed to be accurate but do not override actual proposal. This info is for comparison purposes only

Performance data shown represents past performance. Past performance does not guarantee future results. Investment return and principal value of an investment in fund(s) will fluctuate so that an investor's shares when redeemed may be worth more or less than their original cost. Composite performance data shown is calculated net of fees and reflects any reinvestment of dividends and other distributions and the deduction of fees and expenses.

Source: www.firmcmx.fiduciarymanagement.com

With this kind of report, the analysis becomes a simple visual comparison that could be easily understood by nearly anyone.

I recently responded to a request for proposal or RFP from a local non-profit organization. They had locations in three different major cities in a close regional area. There were approximately 400 employees and multiple job sites in the three cities. The committee felt that the employees were not getting enough service and wanted to see this change.

After evaluating various vendors, I determined that the Principal Financial Group had a great platform with a very high service model. Their website supported a large number of additional tools, but most importantly, they had plan metrics for how often the services were accessed and what was done. This information would help guide me in how I would directly provide education and assistance. I would also incorporate two emails per month, one on the economy, and one on a general topic of interest.

It was important that I also be able to connect with any of the employees on Facebook and LinkedIn to provide them with information when, where, and how they wanted to access it. A calendar of quarterly meetings was created that covered all three major cities, which would be available to all employees, regardless of which location was closest. This would make it possible for people to attend the meetings most convenient for them. I would also be available, by request, for in-person meetings or phone conferences.

This sponsor chose to go another way. I heard feedback through one of the committee members that they really liked what I proposed, but another firm offered personal meetings with all 400 employees, so they decided to go with that firm.

That firm offered individual annuities to each participant, meaning participants would no longer get the benefits of the total value of all of their investments combined; everything would be based on their own account values, and they would be locked into whatever term contract they chose, incurring additional—significant—fees.

Often, these individual annuities come with five-, seven-, or even ten-year surrender schedules and with commissions paid to the advisor of 6% to 12%. In essence, everybody would be doing their own thing and paying the price for it. I believe this most likely doubled or even tripled the cost to the participants. Those fees multiplied by years of investment would likely lead to thousands—maybe hundreds of thousands—of dollars in lost retirement income. I wonder if the committee had been shown an easy-to-understand comparison of the long-term projected costs, would they still have chosen this option.

Another thing to keep in mind when comparing vendors is to not look at averages. Average fund expenses don't mean anything. First, the S & P 500 never returns its average; it is rarely even within half a percentage of it. Second, and my favorite example of why not to use averages, is that the average age of a person wearing diapers is 42.

You need to look at weighted fund expenses based on where the money is actually invested. This will help you understand what is actually being paid by the plan participants. You would be surprised by how many times I see a few index funds thrown into a line-up so that the average fund expense is lowered and helps make it look more attractive. If none of the money is invested there, it is very misleading. What's worse, if the owner and the other highly compensated employees have their money invested there, and the other employees don't, you could end up with a serious problem.

First, the employees may not understand the cost difference, and this puts you at risk. Also, if plan expenses are covered by revenues received from the mutual funds within the plan, this could cause the employees to pay nearly all of the expenses, while the owner and other informed individuals get by with paying hardly anything. This clearly constitutes another potential breach of fiduciary duties and places you at significant personal risk.

Evaluating Advisors

When you are considering what advisor to hire, or whether to retain the advisor you already have, be careful and be diligent. Google your advisor, check them out on www.brightscope.com, and look them up on LinkedIn and Facebook. Information about their background and qualifications is also available at FINRA's website www.brokercheck.finra.org.

Ask yourself, "Does this seem like the kind of person with whom I would want to do business?" Check out their educational background and professional experience and credentials. Find out how much of their business is in the 401(k) space or other employer-sponsored retirement plans. Ask them to share with you their well-designed process and documentation procedure. Look at the services they have provided and how they are delivered. For instance, do they provide educational support? Is this only through prints of materials from the vendor, or do they only conduct group meetings on site once a year? How many employees show up for these meetings? Does the vendor use email; videos; webinars; Facebook, LinkedIn, and other social media to reach employees where they are, at times that are convenient for them? Is information delivered in a manner that is utilized by employees? Is the vendor willing to make special concessions that you request or feel would be valuable? This could include three onsite meetings a year, and quarterly fund performance updates, etc.

Find out what the advisor does to stay current with industry trends and regulatory changes. Are they continuing their education every year? If so how? How much do they charge? Keep in mind, as I have been saying throughout this book that cheaper is not always better. What tools and resources do they bring to the table? What types of fiduciary services do you want; 3(21), 3(38), 3(16), etc.? If they offer these specialty services, how big is the company that backs them? It doesn't do any good to have an advisor provide 3(38) investment services if the firm is only worth a few million dollars. When lawsuits start flying, you generally want a large organization with very deep pockets protecting you, or at least, on the hook with you.

Other factors to consider when evaluating advisors are the way they deliver services, as well as how they charge or get paid for those services. Many financial advisors become the agent or broker-of-record and receive compensation based on the amount of assets within your company's plan, but this might not be the best option for your organization.

I recently worked with the head of the human resources department at a regional bank. She didn't want an advisor as broker-of-record because they owned their own investment firm and the head of HR didn't want the advisor working on the plan to end up pursuing the bank employees. She did realize, however, that the board of directors needed council and guidance with regard to their plan; that's why she reached out to me. She wanted to hire me, on a quoted fee for service, as a paid consultant to the board of directors with regard to the plan operations. For this organization, this approach was what they felt was most beneficial.

Employee Communication

It's important to accurately convey to employees the process of how services are delivered. I have been conducting 401(k) meetings for years, and hundreds of participants have told me that they cannot afford to save because they don't have enough money.

When asked, "What does your budget look like?" Generally all of them can tell me what their monthly bills look like, and how they are careful about how they spend their paychecks.

However, when asked specifically how much they spent on groceries in the last six months and on fuel over the same period. Very, very few can answer these questions.

Many times there are variations in spending based on things that regularly change, like food and fuel. Things might be a little tighter this summer than last winter because they are eating more fresh fruit, and fuel has gone up by 60 cents a gallon. You don't generally see these changes when looking at monthly spending.

Another area that surprises people is the amount they spend on entertainment from month to month. This varies depending on what month it is. I encourage employees to use some kind of money-management system like Quicken® that can help them track their income and expenses. It can help them create a budget and review differences over time. The longer they use it, the more information they have to guide them.

Next, how does the advisor present the information on how to start or increase saving in the plan? I often hear advisors tell employees to save 1% or increase their savings by 1%. Guess what. Nobody does it. Why is that? One percent isn't a number that employees relate to. It is just too vague.

When employees are asked, if they could start saving for retirement later and potentially have an additional $173 per month in retirement, would they do it? Nearly everyone says, "Yes."

When asked if they would miss just one penny out of every dollar they make. I haven't heard anyone say they would. I then close with, "Tomorrow I want you to change your retirement savings by just 1%." Now they understand and can relate to this change.

I also encourage them to take part of the money from any future raises they get and save it in their 401(k) plan. Many who do this will, in a few years, be successfully saving 15% of their pay and not even missing it. The best part is that this level of savings rate, if started soon enough, not only allows them to retire, but most likely they'll retire early, or better yet, be able to do more things in retirement.

Service Selection

It is important that you consider your unique situation, your wants, and your willingness to pay for them when planning your retirement options. I suggest starting by ensuring that you are being provided with a proven, successful, and documentable process. Make sure that it uses individual and impartial evaluation methods and is easy to understand. You should also be provided with a sample investment policy statement against which you can measure and confirm compliance. You should ensure that educational support is offered in a manner convenient for and actually utilized by your employees. Ongoing consultation on how to continually help the company and its employees should be a key part of the overall process.

Does the website offer ease of use? What additional tools are available? Is there an employee assistance program that helps support knowledge and use of all benefits offered by your company? Are there additional resources available to help your employees determine if they are on track to achieving a confident retirement when their time comes? Can the employees engage in personal financial planning that is custom-built to their unique goals, dreams, and timeline? Will the advisor maintain and archive documentation as well as supply a copy to you?

You should also consider whether the services provided are able to help employees deal with the risks they face? This includes emotional risk, market risk, performance risk, inflation risk, and longevity risk. It is very easy to make investing look hard, but it is very hard to make investing look easy.

In the end, the services you select will have an impact on the fees charged. If you work with me, my promise to you is that I will always seek to be competitive on price, but I will not be the low-cost leader.

The Mistakes Plan Sponsors Make When Managing Their 401(k)

Many plan sponsors don't follow the legal requirements. I became a plan advisor for a plan for a small company with only three employees. I was working through things with the employer, when I found out that the company was not making contributions to the plan at the time of payroll, or even reasonably close.

I explained to the employer that these funds needed to be remitted right away. That in fact, she had taken an interest-free loan from her employees without their consent, and that she was not following the employees' direction of investment and the associated returns they would get from that investment. I further explained that there was a voluntary correction program and that this problem could be easily remedied. Unbelievably, her response was, "Just don't tell anyone," And sadly she also wasn't allowing participants to get statements, even if they called the vendor directly. Needless to say, I didn't keep that plan. I don't even want to think about the ramifications and cost to this plan's sponsor in the event of an audit.

Many plan sponsors do not have a developed and documented process. According to W. Andrew Larson the Firestone Supreme Court case determined that if you have a well-thought-out, documented, and followed process, the courts would assume that the plan sponsor acted prudently. I interpret this to mean that the courts and the Department of Labor are not concerned with the results, but rather with the process.

Once I worked with a local company to benchmark their plan. We reviewed all of the criteria for which they were searching and looked at an array of vendors that were willing to supply the desired services, their platforms, and their costs.

The committee, which consisted of general employees as well as the owners and senior management of the company, chose The Standard Insurance Company. They wanted to review their plan investments annually using performance rankings as a criterion, but they absolutely did not want to establish an investment policy statement (IPS). The plan trustees were concerned that if they had an IPS, and didn't or weren't able to follow it, they would be in worse trouble. I advised them that their logic was sound and that this would be worse than not having the statement at all. I also explained that the DOL doesn't require one, but that it would be one of the documents requested in the event of an audit.

I pointed out that there would need to be some criteria used when evaluating and making decisions. How would the committee receive instructions from the plan trustees on what to look at and how to evaluate materials? How would they stay consistent from one meeting to the next? If criteria changed for the evaluation, who would know, and how would it be known? In the end, this organization felt it would still be better to just thoroughly document their meetings and not have the IPS.

Voluntary Corrections

We all know that mistakes happen, and that's okay. The government doesn't expect perfection, and it has provided relief through voluntary fiduciary correction programs. Depending on the type of error, voluntary correction should always be sought out as soon as possible. The consequences are far worse if you get caught through an audit instead.

Here are some examples of what is eligible for this program according to the DOL website:

*delinquent participant contributions and participant loan repayments to pension plans,

*delinquent participant contributions to insured welfare plans,

*delinquent participant contributions to welfare plan trusts,

*fair-market interest rate loans to parties in interests,

*low-market interest rate loans to parties in interests,

*below-market interest rate loans to non-parties in interests,

*below-market interest rate loans due to delay in perfecting security interest,

*participant loans failing to comply with plan provisions for amount duration or level maturation,

*defaulted participant loans,

*purchase of assets by plans for parties in interests,

*sale of assets by plans to parties in interest,

*sale and leaseback property to sponsoring employers,
*purchases of assets from non-parties in interest at more than fair market value,
*sale of assets to non-parties in interest at less than fair market value,
*holding of a liquid asset previously purchased by plan,
*benefit payments based on improper valuation of plan assets,
*payment of duplicate, excessive or unnecessary compensation,
*improper payment of expenses by plan,
*payment of dual compensation to plan fiduciaries.

A calculator is available to help you determine the cost of the remedies at www.dol.gov/ebsa/calculator. You can find out more about the voluntary fiduciary correction program at www.dol.gov/ebsa/newsroom/fs2006vfcp.html.

Common Pitfalls

Not following the developed process that was established can turn into the worst situation for a plan sponsor. If the sponsor recognizes the need for a process and creates it, but does not follow it, they will most likely be found liable to the plan participants, regardless of what the participants chose to do. Not following the developed process basically eliminates the protections offered under ERISA to the plan sponsor and is generally considered a breach of fiduciary duty, which puts the plan sponsor's personal assets at risk.

Imagine sitting down at a poker table and playing with your entire retirement account balance. Is that something you would be willing to do or think is prudent? If the plan sponsor is not following the developed process, this may be the best thing for the participant to do. You see, if the sponsor isn't following the established process or not meeting all the requirements under section 404(c) to get the protections it affords the plan fiduciaries, the individual participant could very well be doing the right thing. If they win, they make a lot of money. If they lose, they can file a complaint with the Department of Labor or hire an attorney and pursue the employer to regain their lost money, plus a court-mandated annual return. They would most likely get it. Section 404(c) regulations provide relief from liability to a plan fiduciary for investment decisions made by the retirement plan participants who have the ability to exercise control over their investments, provided certain other conditions are all met.

The Retirement Learning Center has put together this checklist to help you evaluate your 404(c) compliance status:

____ **Yes** ____ **No.** Has the plan provided the participant with the required participant information? In order to Satisfy the information that, generally, would be sufficient to enable the participant to make informed investment decisions. Information that must be provided includes the following:

1. An explanation that the plan is intended to be a 404(c) plan
2. An explanation that the fiduciaries may be relieved of liability.
3. A description of each investment alternative available under the plan, which can be general when the plan permits any investment, but should encourage participants to review information on the investment.
4. Each designated alternative must include a general description of the investment objectives and risk and return characteristics, and information regarding the type and diversification of assets in the portfolio of the designated alternative.
5. The identity of any designated investment manager.
6. An explanation of the circumstances under which participants may give investment instructions including limitations on such instructions; restrictions on transfer; limitation on voting rights; and information on penalties or adjustments related to fund transfers
7. A description of transaction fees and expenses chargeable against the participants account.
8. Information on indemnification of the plan fiduciary responsible for giving information on request.

9. Information regarding investments in employer securities including a description of the procedure to provide for confidentiality and identity of the fiduciary charged with monitoring compliance with the confidentiality requirement.
10. A copy of most recent prospectus provided to the plan if the investment is subject to the Securities Act of 1933 (this can be given immediately before or after investment).
11. After investment, participants must be provided with plan materials related to the exercise of voting, tender, or similar rights. If there are plan provisions regarding the exercise of such rights, participants must receive a description of or reference to such rights, Section 404(c) relief is not available to the extent that the plan fiduciaries exercise the rights.

___Yes ___No. If requested by the participant, does the plan provide the information that must be available upon participant request? Participant must be provided certain information upon request. This material must be based on the latest information available to the plan, and includes the following

1. A narrative of the annual operating expenses of each designated investment alternative, including investment manager fees, administrative fees, and transaction costs, which reduce the rate of return to the participant. The aggregate of such expenses must be expressed as a

percentage of average net assets of the designated investment alternative. If the information is already in the prospectus, providing the prospectus is sufficient.

2. Copies of prospectuses, financial statements and reports, and other materials related to the investment alternatives to the extent the information is provided to the plan.
3. Regarding the designated investment alternatives: (a) a list of assets comprising the portfolio of the alternative that includes plan assets and the value of the assets, and (b) if the asset is a fixed rate investment contract, the name of the issues of the contract, the term of the contract, and the rate of return on the contract.
4. The value of shares or units and past and current investment performance of each available alternative, net of expenses.
5. The value of the shares or units held in the particular participants account.

___ **Yes** ___**No.** Does the plan provide the necessary participant information in a timely manner? The plan must provide the required participant information before assets are invested. The plan must provide other information in sufficient time for the participant to consider the information prior to making an investment.

___ **Yes** ___ **No.** Does the plan carry out participant investment instructions? The plan must follow the participant's investment instructions, unless the instructions would cause the plan to create a prohibited transaction, or would generate income taxable to the plan. The fiduciary is not relieved of liability when a participant instruction, if implemented would:

1. Not be in accordance with the plan document
2. Cause the indicia of ownership of plan assets to be outside the U.S
3. Jeopardize the plan's tax qualified status
4. Plausibly result in a loss in excess of a participant's account balance.
5. Result in a prohibited transaction

Since the plan fiduciary is not relieved of fiduciary responsibility in the above events, it can decline to carry out investment instructions that would cause them.

___ **Yes** ___**No.** Do participants have the ability to change their investments as often as the volatility of investments may require (and at least quarterly)? Plans must give participants the opportunity to change their investments as often as the volatility of the investments may require, and at least every three months.

___ **Yes** ___ No. Does the plan offer a broad range of investment alternatives? The investment lineup for the plan must be sufficient enough to permit participants a reasonable opportunity to materially affect the potential risk and returns on their investments. The participants must also have an opportunity to choose from at least three investments that meet the following criteria:

1. Are diversified
2. Have materially different risk and return characteristics
3. In the aggregate, enable the participant to achieve aggregate risk and return characteristics at any point within the range "normally appropriate for the participant."
4. Each of which, when combined with the other alternatives, tends to minimize, through diversification, the overall risk of the portfolio.

All of the above must be answered yes for the plan to be ERISA 404(c) compliant."

Source: Columbia Threadneedle Retirement Learning Center What is ERISA sec. 404(c) protection", 2011

Another mistake that plan sponsors make is not paying reasonable fees or overpaying. If the sponsor chooses to keep their existing plan vendor and advisor, even while knowing that they could get a substantial discount by opting for something at the same level of service or higher, they are not meeting the reasonable standard.

Recently, I did a review for a company that didn't really want to change anything but recognized that they hadn't done any evaluation or benchmarking to their plan. The plan had grown to a few million dollars, and better pricing was potentially available. Gathering all of the relevant information, I contacted various vendors to see what their pricing would look like. There was over 40% in potential cost savings based on what other service providers were willing to host the plan for.

Then I worked with the plan sponsor to contact their existing provider, shared the information I had compiled, and asked them if they would like to submit a new pricing proposal to retain the business. They returned a couple of days later with new pricing that was right in line with what the market was willing to do, and the company would not even have to change vendors. The plan sponsor was ecstatic. The long-term benefits to his employees will most likely result in significantly higher account balances at retirement due to the long-term effect of these cost savings.

If this company had decided it didn't want to change anything, it would not have gotten this reduction in fees and would still be paying way too much. Would that company be willing to overpay one of its vendors or its employees by that much? If not, how can it say that it's operating the plan in the best interest of the participants?

What if it was using employee balances to make loans to its customers? What if it argued that this helped employees have jobs? Would an outsider looking in think that this was prudent or in the best interest of the participants? I still can't believe this really happened.

A plan sponsor should also provide adequate information to participants, so they can make informed decisions. One mistake that often occurs is when employees are investing their retirement money in mutual funds when they don't know how these investments work. There is a ton of information on the vendor website about these funds. Access to the prospectus, which is the legal document on how the funds operate, past performance for the current time period, as well as one-, three-, five-, and even ten-year periods are generally also available. You can also find a list of holdings within the fund, as well as information about the manager, etc. However, if an employee doesn't know what a mutual fund is, do you think they have enough information to make an informed decision?

Lastly, some plan sponsors make the mistake of setting up employees for failure. If you know that your employees are not saving enough to retire, how is that in their best interest? Through plan design, you could set up auto-enroll and auto-escalate to help them on the path to retirement? Maybe you could offer a stretch match to help encourage employees to save more. Or establish and convey corporate goals that could result in a profit sharing which is a discretionary amount and determined after the fact. Of course, the employee can make the decision to intentionally not save enough for retirement by opting out, but this active decision relieves the plan sponsor of their responsibility for the decision.

The Great 8 Myths

Over the years I have come across many misperceptions, half-truths or outright misunderstandings. I like to call them The Great 8 Myths.

Myth #1 is that cheapest is always better. The problem is, how do you determine which plan is cheapest? Also, cheap implies poor quality; therefore, "inexpensive" would be the better word choice, as it implies good value for fees paid.

A few years ago I received a request for proposal from an investment consultant who was handling the process for a hospital, which had a couple of different plans that served the different needs of the participants within their organization with well over $250,000,000 in total assets. As part of their process they received bids from various vendors to operate the plan directly with them and have no outside advisor. However, we recommended Mass Mutual Financial Group®. My team included two other advisors with offices just a few blocks away from both of the hospital's locations in neighboring towns. Our proposal was a bit more expensive than the other proposals; thus, we were not selected. What the selection committee hadn't considered was that the head of human resources and her number-two person were spending incredible amounts of time handling issues related to the plan. This included creating materials and running group meetings for the employees. The salaries of these two individuals were more than the additional cost we had proposed. These individuals were also not licensed and may have been doing some things that placed them, and their organization, at risk under ERISA. Furthermore, they had other tasks to do for the organization and were overwhelmed by their workload.

This cheaper offering actually provided less support, exposing the organization to possible risk and was likely more expensive when factoring in the cost that the hospital was directly paying in the salaries of those two HR personnel.

Myth #2 Working with a large company assures you the best plan. In May of 2015, I was searching through the 5500 filings on the Department of Labor's website and came across a medical clinic with a few doctors I knew. As a larger plan, they were required to file a more detailed report, which included an accounting audit. I noticed that their fidelity bond seemed to be less than what might be needed. The amount of the bond is generally required to be at least 10% of plan assets, up to $500,000 for each plan fiduciary. I knew that the clinic had an investment committee with at least a few members, plus a director and at least one support staff person involved in the control and oversight of the plan and its assets, and this was the basis for my concern.

Conducting an in-depth analysis of the funds they had available within the plan and its cost, I found that they could have saved an estimated $35,000 per year. I also noticed that they were making a fairly substantial contribution to their employees and realized that if this was at least 5% or higher, the clinic might be a good candidate for a cash balance plan. Since there were a large number of doctors, they might not even have to include any of their regular employees while allowing the doctors to sock away possibly an extra few hundred thousand dollars a year into their retirement accounts. These contributions would, of course, reduce the doctors' current income, which could have a dramatic impact on their tax situations, especially given all the new taxes that took effect in 2013. These assets would also most likely be sheltered from loss and bankruptcy under the protection afforded ERISA plans.

Unfortunately, the clinic's director would not even agree to a meeting. She was sure that there was nothing wrong with their plan and that there were no improvements that could be made.

Myth #3 Employees cannot afford to save enough for retirement. Many employees and employers tell me all the time that they cannot afford to save for retirement. What they are really saying is that they are living at the level that 100% of their wages will support. If they have to live on 100% now, how are they going to retire in the future on 75% to 85% of their total wages? Many also say they'll start saving in the future, maybe after they have been married for a while or after the kids finish college. There's always something competing for those dollars.

Let's say they actually start saving 15% of their pay when they are 40 years old. If they are making $40,000 a year at that time, they will save $6,000 a year for the next 27 years until 67, the age of retirement. Assuming a long-term stock market average, which nobody ever actually makes, of 8% per year, would grow into $566,033.

Let's compare that to someone who starts saving at 25 years of age and only makes $25,000 a year. This pay will increase by about 2% annually. They only save 3% of their pay but increase that savings rate by 1% every other year until they are saving 15% of their pay. They may decide to retire early at age 62 with $637,201. Or maybe they wait until age 67 and end up with $989,627 (assuming the same 8% growth rate on their investments.)

Now, let's look at the person who didn't save anything. They will likely have nothing and be unable to retire. Maybe they were able to buy a house and pay for it over the years, but now it's the only asset they have, so they may be put in the position of needing to sell it or take a reverse mortgage to fund their retirement.

People can't afford not to save for retirement, especially since the number-one fear I hear from employees, clients, and prospective clients is to be alive, yet broke during retirement. I haven't even factored in that according to the social security 2016 trustees report, starting in 2019, interest income and redemption of trust fund asset reserves from the General Fund of the Treasury will provide the resources needed to offset Social Security's annual deficits until 2034, when the reserves will be depleted. Thereafter, scheduled tax income is projected to be sufficient to pay about three-quarters of scheduled benefits through the end of the projection period in 2090. The ratio of reserves to one year's projected cost (the combined trust fund ratio) peaked in 2008, declined through 2015, and is expected to decline steadily until the trust funds are depleted in 2034[1]. I interpret this to mean that I may or may not ever get any benefits paid to support my retirement under this program.

Myth #4 There are no adverse impacts to an employer when an employee cannot afford to retire. Not true. How do the younger employees get to advance their careers and increase their earnings if no one is retiring because they cannot afford to do so? Older workers generally have higher wages and a higher cost of health care. Many employers provide assistance through group health plans by

[1] www.ssa.gov/oact/trsum/

paying some, or all, of the health insurance premiums for employees. I've seen recent estimates of additional cost to the employer of $5,000 per year for each non-retired employee. This doesn't even take into account the cost of the younger employees quitting their jobs to take advancement opportunities at other companies.

Money is generally cited as one of the main sources of stress for individuals. It is often considered one of the irreconcilable differences that can become the basis for divorce. It often causes distraction at work, which can lead to accidents and poor performance. Do you think your employees are able to focus on their jobs if they are worried about their money?

Myth #5 One of the potential adverse costs of a 401(k) plan occurs when a company buys another company that also has a 401(k) plan. Since most advisors serving small businesses aren't 401(k) specialists, they don't understand the risk this poses.

Let's say your business has been doing really well, but you would like to expand into a neighboring town or state. The easiest way to do so is to buy an existing business in your targeted area that is already doing what you are doing and seeking to expand. They have a healthy balance sheet and a good management team.

You buy them, and combine their 401(k) into yours. Everything in the company is going great; business is up, profits are up, and the future is full of possibilities. Then you conduct your annual plan review (which now includes the merged plan) and find out that there has been no process, documentation, analysis or oversight of any kind on the old company's plan for years.

Participants haven't been getting required notices, the fees were nearly double, the investment line-up hadn't changed since the plan was started over ten years ago, etc. Now you and your company are on the hook for any and all fiduciary breaches, even though they were done by the purchased company.

You might be thinking that this cannot be true, but it is. I cannot stress enough the importance of consulting your advisor, regardless of what the company is doing. In this scenario I would have advised you to review the plan ahead of time and most likely terminate that plan and allow the employees to choose to roll over their assets to your company's plan so that any and all past breaches do not become your future responsibility.

Another cost sometimes occurs when the owner, and the highly compensated employees, are saving aggressively into their plan and cause it to become top-heavy. The government wants these plans to be fair, and this is one of the ways by which they determine that. If you do not have a safe harbor plan which includes a vested contribution to the employee, then this test can force you to make a contribution to the employees to meet the fairness determination. This is definitely not what you want to be told after the first of the year when you are working on completing your testing and 5500 filing.

Overall, plan compliance problems can be time consuming and expensive. As I mentioned at the beginning of this book, there are significant sums paid in reimbursements to employee accounts, and let's not forget the potential criminal ramifications.

The attorney fees alone for dealing with these issues can be staggering.

It's okay not to document your actions, but if you don't, how will you explain to a DOL or IRS auditor, or the courts, in the event of a lawsuit. They will expect to be shown the what, when, where, how and why something was done. How will you even remember? If you reviewed investments, what criteria did you use, and what decisions were made? If you are being sued, these considerations are after the fact. They know the results of performance on the investments. If they didn't perform well, and the employees lost money, they want someone to blame and to give the employees their money back. If you cannot show what your reasoning was, and that you followed a diligent process in determining what funds to offer, you are exposed to the risk of making up those losses to all of the plan participants. Is that a risk you want to take?

Myth #6 Small plans don't have to worry about being audited because the IRS and the DOL only go after the big boys. Awhile back I was contacted by a building contractor. He wanted to know if I could help him because he had received an investigation notice from the Department of Labor. He only had a few employees and not even $1 million in his plan.

I asked him a bit about his procedures, documentation, and investments. He didn't have any of the first two things, and he had been making direct real estate investments with pretty much all of the money. I told him that there wasn't really anything I could do about how he had handled things in the past and that I wouldn't be able to take him on as a client, given his current circumstances. I advised him to find a good ERISA attorney and wished him the best of luck.

Myth #7 As a plan sponsor, your fiduciary obligation is passed to the advisors you hire. This couldn't be further from the truth. I have asked many plan sponsors about their policy procedures and documentation, and they respond, "My advisor handles that," "My third-party administrator takes care of that," or, "Doesn't my vendor handle that?" All of these parties may be involved—they may even have some responsibility—but as the plan sponsor, you can only share your responsibility, you can't eliminate it.

I recently met with a plan sponsor to begin a comprehensive review of their plan. When I met with the person who was signing the 5500, she told me she couldn't remember what documents I would need. As we were walking to her office, I started to list them off: Investment Policy Statement, 408(b)2 or 405(a) fee statements, copies of last year's committee meeting minutes....at this point she interrupted me and said, "I don't know what any of those are. We just send our money to Fidelity." As we sat down in her office, I inquired as to who their advisor was and how often he reviewed things with them and conducted meetings for the employees. Turns out he was in an entirely different state and didn't conduct any meetings for them or the employees. I pointed out that she was a plan fiduciary and that any breaches of her fiduciary obligations placed her at personal risk. "We will just shut this plan down right now!" she proclaimed immediately.

At this point I advised her that was why I was here to meet with her, and that my team and I would provide her the assistance and guidance she needed. We would help them establish a prudent process, follow it, and document it. I also explained that there were service providers that would "share" her responsibilities, and simplify her role enough so she could almost just send the money in. I explained that by having 3(16) administrative services provided along with 3(38) investment advice everything would be taken care of and she would only need to review the work done by these service providers during our annual review.

Myth #8 The plan sponsor is not responsible for the results of the employees' investment decisions. This myth is a little trickier. If you are taking advantage of the protections offered under section 404(c), then this myth would be correct; however, you must meet all the requirements. If you miss even one requirement, you are not able to receive the protections it offers. If, for instance, you don't review your investments on a regular basis and make sure that they are still appropriate to offer, you could end up being liable for employee losses as well as missed gains.

The 401(k) Checkup Works for Many Different Situations

Currently, I work as the advisor for an RV dealership, and I have done so for many years. When the economy was good (before the Great Recession of 2007), the dealership was making contributions and the owners were saving large sums for their own personal retirements.

When the recession hit, they had to drop the profit sharing, which also nearly stopped their ability to save because their plan would become top-heavy. In general, this means that the owners and other key employees had around 60% of the total plan assets in their accounts and would have required a contribution to the non-key employees. Also, the employees weren't saving very much, and so they were having problems with the ACP and ADP testing and were usually getting money back out of the plan because they contributed too much (based on these tests.)

We looked at a bunch of different ways to help them get their retirement savings back on track once the economy recovered, but they still had the same problems. Each year during our review, I recommended that we look at adding auto enrollment. They didn't feel confident doing this and were worried about how the employees would view it. I explained that most employees don't view it negatively, and many companies see 90% or more stay with the savings plan.

They finally amended their plan to include this feature, and they now only have two employees who have opted out. The best part is that they can now start saving for their personal retirements at a faster pace because of the higher savings rate they are now able to achieve under the ACP and ADP tests They also know that they have done what they can to get the employees back on track to achieve successful retirements when their times come.

At one other time I served as an advisor to help establish a new plan for a small medical practice. The owner wanted to jump start her personal retirement savings, which had gotten wiped out because of her battle with breast cancer. Now that she was healthy again, she needed to make up for lost time.

I explained that for her to save her maximum contribution and meet the government's fairness requirements, we would need to "buy" our way out of the fairness tests required by the government by doing a safe harbor contribution. She didn't mind giving 3% of their pay to the employees to be able to do this.

The plan is now up and running, and everyone is participating. Naturally the plan sponsor is ecstatic because she is now able to max out her own retirement savings each year.

Creating a plan for a small but very successful aerospace company for the owners who were paying far too much on their taxes was rewarding for me. The owners were looking for ways to save and I shared the same plan design and idea that I created for the small medical practice with them. The owners loved it. I told them to remember to keep in mind the 3% when they made job offers because it is a fairly significant amount for most of their employees.

Their company and their plan have grown substantially over the past few years, and recently they started an additional company and hired more employees. They feel that their benefits package is a significant part of their success in attracting and retaining the caliber of employees that they need.

The owner of a fast casual food franchise was looking for ways to keep saving for his retirement since his intent was to retire early. He didn't really need the money now, but recognized that early retirement would only be possible if he maxed out his personal contributions each year. We met and discussed the fairness issues and the safe harbor option. He knew his employees all generally worked for minimum wage, were young, and would not really value retirement savings at this time.

He decided to encourage his employees by choosing a safe harbor match where he would match money saved by the employees based on the approved formula. He figured that it might not cost him much because many of the employees likely would not save but he could at least reward those who did.

Currently he continues to max out his contributions every year. He was right about the employees not saving; only he and his manager are actively saving at this time. Still, he's very happy because he is currently looking at a projected early retirement at age 55.

How to Get Your Prescription for a Successful 401(k)

You already know how complex today's benefit programs are while trying to help your employees reach their retirement income goals. The confusing part is staying up on all the changes in requirements under ERISA while you are busy running your company or department so you aren't at risk of being out of compliance.

Start by answering these three questions:

How Important	Where It Is Now	Desired Outcome
1.		
2.		
3.		
4.		
5.		

Next evaluate your company's plan.

1. Do you feel that you are meeting all your legal obligations?
2. Have you documented your actions and archived these records?
3. How much are you, your company, and your employees paying?
4. Are these fees "reasonable"?

5. Do you know what role/services are being provided for each of your contracted providers?
6. Will your employees be able to successfully retire when the time comes?
7. How are you providing education to help your employees make informed decisions?

Next, begin your 401(k) check-up, by visiting **www.The401KCheck.com**. There you will find directions on how to submit a request for your 401(k) checkup, including the documents you need to supply, where to send them, and how to contact me.

Initially, I will conduct an interview with you and your company management to discuss what you have, what you would like to have, and the things that you could have. Based on this, I'll develop a written analysis and comparison of your existing plan, propose a list of services to be performed, and create a schedule to deliver those services based on what and when you want them. Next, I will provide a documentable process for you to follow, determining who, what, when, where, why, and how, and help you stick to it. I will also create and maintain an archive for this documentation.

By requesting a consultation or second opinion on any aspect of your 401(k), you will not only be meeting your requirements under ERISA, but you will also obtain an independent analysis of what you are doing, what you are paying, and what you are getting for those fees, along with ways to improve and/or reduce cost.

Steps to Get Your Prescription for a Successful 401(k)

My team and I will work with you to perform a 401(k) checkup to ensure your 401(k) is in compliance by following these simple steps:

Step 1: We will conduct a thorough independent analysis and comparison of your existing plan. This will include: what you are doing, what you are paying and what you are getting for the fees you are paying. You will need to submit copies of your summary plan description, Investment Policy Statement, investment committee meeting minutes for prior year, 408(b)2 and/or 405(a) fee disclosure forms, last annual review, list of current assets and which investments they are in and thru which provider. I will also need about 30-minutes of your time for a personal interview to gather the remaining information needed.

Step 2: From this we will develop a proven, successful and documentable process for you to follow. We will help ensure that you stick to it and will archive the documentation to prove it. Additionally, we will show you ways to improve or reduce your costs while increasing your 401(k) checkup score.

Step 3: We take it from here and monitor and advise you on diversified plan options to maintain ERISA compliance and help minimize risk.

Most plan sponsors spend a lot of time and energy when they first setup their plan but then spend all their time running their company, possibly allowing their 401(k) to fall out of ERISA compliance.

Now you can get your prescription for a successful 401(k) by having your own 401(k) Checkup.

If you have questions or would like us to help, call me at 541-659-5112 or visit **www.the401KCheck.com.**

I can also be reached via email at **Rick@the401kCheck.com**, and we will take it from there.

The Standard & Poor's 500 Index (S&P 500® Index), an unmanaged index of common stocks, is frequently used as a general measure of market performance. The index reflects reinvestment of all distributions and changes in market prices, but excludes brokerage commissions or other fees.

Glossary of Terms

The Language of Retirement Plans Glossary Invesco Plan*Forward* Foundations℠

Understanding employer-sponsored, tax-qualified retirement plans is easier when you know the terminology.

12(b)-1 fee
A cost charged to shareholders to pay for a mutual fund's distribution and marketing costs.

3(16) Plan Fiduciary
See *ERISA* on page 89 for definition.

3(21) Advising Fiduciary
See *ERISA* on page 89 for definition.

3(38) Managing Fiduciary
See *ERISA* on page 89 for definition.

401(k) plan
An employer-sponsored defined contribution plan that allows participants to defer part of their compensation on a pretax basis to save for retirement. 401(k) refers to the section of the Internal Revenue Code (IRC) that describes this arrangement. 401(k) plans are often referred to as "cash or deferred arrangements" (CODA).

402(g) limits (employee elective deferral limits)
The maximum amount of elective deferral contributions a participant may make to any employer-sponsored, tax-qualified retirement

plan(s). The 402(g) limit is an annual individual limit covering all deferral contributions regardless of plan(s). All elective deferral contributions to any tax-qualified retirement plan are subject to 402(g) limits, which are adjusted annually to reflect increases in the cost of living (COLA). (Also see catch-up contributions on page 82.)

403(b) arrangement
An annuity contract or custodial account that meets the requirements of Section 403(b) of the IRC. Only employees of certain public schools, universities and tax-exempt organizations described in section 501(c) (3) of the IRC are eligible to establish 403(b) arrangements. The Treasury Department issued final 403(b) regulations that will cause administrative changes in the way current 501(c)(3) organizations, churches, schools and hospitals do business.

404 limit – employer deductible contribution limit
The maximum annual deduction permitted by an employer for federal income tax purposes with respect to tax-qualified, retirement plan contributions (employer contributions). 404 refers to the section of the IRC that sets the limit. Separate limits apply to defined contribution plans and defined benefit plans. The defined contribution limit is an aggregate limit covering all contributions by an employer to any defined contribution plan(s). The annual defined contribution plan deduction limit is 25% of eligible compensation earned by all plan participants for that year.

404(c) regulations
Regulations that relieve a plan fiduciary of liability for investment decisions made by retirement plan participants who have the ability to exercise control over their plan account investments, provided certain other conditions are met. Compliance with 404(c) is optional.

408(b)(2)
See *ERISA* on page 89 for definition.

415 limit – annual additions limit
The annual contribution limit to a participant account. This limit includes all contributions except rollover and loan repayment. 415 refers to the section of the IRC that sets the limit. Separate limits apply to defined contribution plans and defined benefit plans. The defined contribution limit is an aggregate limit. All annual additions to the account of a participant - under all tax-qualified defined contribution retirement plan(s) maintained by the employer - are counted against the limit. The annual defined contribution plan 415 limit for a year is generally the lesser of 100% of the participant's eligible compensation for a year or a specified dollar limit, which is adjusted annually to reflect changes in the cost of living.

Common Types of Contributions
All contributions count toward a participant's annual addition limit:

- Designated Roth contributions. Also known as Roth 401(k) contributions, these are elective deferrals currently included in gross income. Qualifying distributions made from designated Roth accounts, including the earnings on designated Roth contributions, are tax free.

- Discretionary (or profit sharing) (nonelective). A nonmandatory amount paid by the employer in accordance with the terms of the plan
- Elective deferrals. A participant's voluntary pretax contribution in accordance with the terms of his or her retirement plan
- Forfeiture reallocation. A reallocation of assets resulting from attrition in the work place

457 plan
A deferred compensation arrangement sponsored by a federal, state or local government/municipality or a tax-exempt organization. Most 457 plans are funded by elective deferrals and are similar to 401(k) plans (but significantly different tax rules apply). 457 refers to the section of the IRC that describes the tax treatment of 457 plans.

ACP test
Actual contribution percentage test. *See ADP/ACP nondiscrimination tests* on page 62.

Active Management
Where a person or team, often called the portfolio manager, actively makes investment decisions and initiates buying and selling of securities using analytical research, forecasts, and their own judgment and experience. The opposite of active management is called passive management, better known as "indexing."

Active share
A measure of how different a fund's portfolio is from its benchmark, determined by comparing the stocks held and their weightings with those of the benchmark.

Administrator
The party responsible for managing the day-to-day activities of the plan. This is often the plan sponsor. The plan sponsor may delegate these duties to a third party.

Administration and recordkeeping expenses
Fees for administrative and recordkeeping services pertaining to plan participants. For start-up or takeover plans, these fees typically include charges associated with processing information from the previous service provider and mapping participant information.

Adoption agreement
The portion of the plan document that contains all of the alternatives and options that may be selected by the employer.

ADP test
Actual deferral percentage test. See *ADP/ACP nondiscrimination tests* below.

ADP/ACP nondiscrimination tests
Nondiscrimination tests that apply to 401(k) plans. The ADP test prohibits highly compensated employees (HCE) from making disproportionately greater elective deferral contributions to a 401(k) plan than nonhighly compensated employees (NHCE). The ACP test prohibits HCEs from making employee after-tax contributions and receiving

employer matching contributions in disproportionately greater amounts than NHCEs.

Age-weighted allocation
A profit sharing allocation formula designed to provide a greater benefit to older participants. (Also see profit sharing plan on page 89.)

Allocation
The amount credited to a participant's account as a result of employer and employee contributions, forfeitures and investment earnings.

Alpha
An expression of performance that measures the difference between a fund's actual returns and its expected performance given its level of risk as measured by beta.

Alternative investments
An investment that is not one of the three traditional asset types: stocks, bonds and cash. Some examples of alternative investments include hedge funds, managed futures, real estate, commodities and derivatives contracts.

Annual annuity fee
Fee charged for the distribution of plan proceeds as annuitized payments.

Annual audit
All plans with more than 100 participants are required by federal law to undergo an annual audit conducted by an independent auditor. A Department of Labor (DOL) or IRS examination of a plan is commonly referred to as a plan audit.

Annuitized payments
A distribution arrangement involving a series of payments made regularly over a specified time period.

Annuity and stable value/GIC surrender charges
Vendors may require that surrender charges be paid if the plan terminates its contract with a provider of annuities or stable value/ GIC (guaranteed investment contract) funds prior to completion of the contract. (Also see Guaranteed investment (interest) contract (GIC) on page 94.) Vendors may also require surrender charges for an individual participant transfer or termination.

Asset allocation
An investment strategy that seeks to balance risk and reward based on apportioning portfolio assets among three main asset classes (equities, fixed income and cash and equivalents, which behave differently over time) according to an individual's goals, risk tolerance and investment horizon. Asset allocation cannot guarantee a profit or protect against loss.

Automatic deferral default percentage
The percentage of pay that is automatically deferred when an employee is enrolled in a plan through automatic enrollment. A typical automatic deferral default percentage is 3% of pay. Generally, participants can choose to defer an amount other than the default percentage.

Automatic enrollment
A plan feature that allows an employer to enroll employees in a salary deferral plan without the

employees' initial consent, as long as employees have the right to "opt out" of contributing to the plan. Also known as "negative election."

Auto escalation
A plan which automatically increases the percentage of (retirement) funds saved from salary. This type of plan generally features a default or standard contribution escalation rate; participants have the right to opt out.

Balance inquiry expense
Fee charged for each participant inquiry about account balance.

Balanced fund
A fund portfolio that combines a stock component, a bond component and, sometimes, a money market component. These hybrid funds generally maintain a relatively fixed mix of stocks and bonds that is either moderate (higher equity component) or conservative (higher fixed-income component).

Basis point (BP)
A unit of measure used to describe the percentage change in the value or rate of a financial instrument. One basis point is one one-hundredth of a percentage point, or 0.01%. If the U.S. Federal Reserve increases its short-term interest rate target by 50 basis points, or a bond's yield rises by 50 basis points, the change would be 0.50% or one-half of one percent.

Benchmarking
A quality assurance tool allowing organizations to compare themselves to others regarding some

aspect of plan design or performance, with a view to finding ways to improve.

Beneficiary
The party designated by a participant — or the terms of a plan — to receive the retirement plan benefits of a deceased participant.

Beta
A measure of volatility, or risk, relative to the index. By definition, the index beta is one. A beta greater than one implies the fund has been more volatile than the index; a beta of less than one implies the fund has been less volatile than the index.

Blackout period
A period during which plan participants cannot access their accounts. A blackout period may occur due to a change in plan providers, record-keepers, trustees or company status, or during the valuation process. The blackout period can also be referred to as lockdown, transitional period or quiet period.

Break in service
Typically, a one-year break in service is defined as a period of 12 consecutive months during which an employee is not credited with more than 500 hours of service.

Bundled services
An arrangement in which plan service providers charge an all-inclusive fee for 401(k) plan establishment, investment services and administration. Bundled services are priced as a package and cannot be priced on a per-service basis.

Cafeteria plan (Section 125)
A plan permitting pretax payment of employee benefits. Section 125 of the IRC defines all benefits that may be paid pretax. Examples of such benefits include health, dental, disability and dependent care.

Catch-up contributions
Contributions that permit individuals 50 or older to make additional elective deferral contributions in excess of the 402(g) limit, the 415 limit or any other limit imposed by the terms of a tax-qualified retirement plan. Catch-up contributions were established by the Economic Growth and Tax Relief Reconciliation Act of 2001 (EGTRRA). The maximum amount of annual catch-up contributions is adjusted annually to reflect increases in the cost of living.

Cliff vesting
A vesting schedule in which the participant's accumulation is not vested during the initial years of service but becomes fully vested upon completing the number of years required by the plan. While traditional vesting schedules are graduated (20%, 40%, 60%, etc.), cliff vesting is not (0%, 0% and 100%).

COLA
Acronym for cost of living adjustment, which refers to periodic (generally annual) changes in wages, benefits or contribution levels. The IRS issues COLAs, which are designed to compensate for the effects of inflation.

Collective trust fund
A tax-exempt, pooled fund, operated by a bank or trust company that commingles assets of trust accounts for which the bank provides fiduciary services. Also known as collective investment trusts.

Commission
A fee paid to a broker or other intermediary for executing a trade.

Compliance testing
Testing required by the IRS to ensure that nonhighly compensated employees (NHCEs) benefit enough from the plan relative to the benefit received by the highly compensated employees (HCEs). (Also see HCE on page 95 and NHCE on page 100.)

Conflict of interest
A conflict between the private interests and the official responsibilities of a person in a position of trust.

Contract administration charge
A charge for administering the insurance/annuity contract, including costs associated with participant account maintenance and all investment-related transactions initiated by participants.

Contract termination charge
A charge to the plan for "surrendering" or "terminating" its insurance/annuity contract prior to the end of a stated time period. The charge typically decreases over time.

Controlled group
When two or more businesses are under common control, meaning one entity owns at least 80% of the stock, profit or capital interest in the other organization, or when the same five or fewer people own a controlling interest in each entity.

Conversion
The process of changing from one service provider to another.

Cross-testing
Generally refers to nondiscrimination testing performed on a defined contribution plan by projecting the contributions to retirement age, converting the projected account balances to monthly benefits and comparing the benefits. Examples of cross-tested plans include age-weighted or new comparability plans.

Custodian
A person or entity that has lawful custody of plan assets for another individual or entity. The custodian's responsibility is to track and hold the plan's securities. Financial institutions — such as trust companies, banks or mutual fund companies — and insurance companies often serve as custodians.

Custody fee
Fee for the safekeeping of plan investments.

DB(k) plan
A defined benefit plan with a salary deferral feature. Beginning in 2010, employers with two to 500

employees when the plan is established may adopt a DB(k) plan.

DCIO

Acronym for the “defined contribution investment only” business, which refers to investment management mandates, awarded within qualified retirement plans such as 401(k), 403(b) and 457 plans.

Defined benefit plan

An employer-sponsored retirement plan that pays a specific amount to a retired employee. The amount to be paid to the retired employee is usually based on a formula that takes salary history and years of service into account. The employer bears the investment risk because the plan promises a specific benefit. If plan assets (including employer contributions and investment earnings) are insufficient to fund benefit payments to plan participants, the employer must generally contribute the difference.

Defined contribution plan

An employer-sponsored retirement plan, such as a 401(k) or profit sharing plan, that is funded by employer contributions, employee elective deferrals or both. Unlike defined benefit plans; the participants bear the investment risk because the plan does not promise a specific benefit. Instead, it promises to pay the employee the amount in his or her account, which is the sum of contributions and investment earnings.

Determination letter
A letter issued by the IRS (upon request) acknowledging that the IRS has reviewed the plan document and determined it to be in compliance. A letter of determination may be relied on as proof of having a qualified plan document in good order.

Direct compensation
Compensation that the service provider receives directly from the plan. This includes payments made directly from the plan for services rendered to the plan or because of a service provider's position with the plan.

Discretionary contributions
Amounts an employer may — but is not obligated to — contribute to a plan. Discretionary contributions can be profit sharing or matching contributions.

Distribution
A lump-sum or periodic payment paid to a participant or beneficiary as required under the terms of a retirement plan.

Distribution expense
The costs typically associated with processing distributions from plan assets to a participant, including required filings (1099 and 945).

Diversification
A risk management technique that mixes a variety of investments within a portfolio. The rationale for this technique is that different kinds of investments will, on average, result in higher returns with lower risk than any individual investment in the portfolio

because positive performance of some investments will neutralize the negative performance of others. Diversification cannot guarantee a profit or protect against loss.

DOL
Acronym for Department of Labor, which enforces legislation that regulates employers who offer pension or welfare benefit plans for their employees. DOL also enforces fiduciary, disclosure and reporting requirements for fiduciaries of pension and welfare benefit plans.

Downside capture ratio
A statistical measure of an investment manager's overall performance in down-markets that is used to evaluate how well the manager performed relative to an index during periods when that index has dropped. The ratio is calculated by dividing the manager's returns by the returns of the index during the down-market and multiplying that factor by 100.

Education program expenses
Costs associated with providing print, video, software and live instruction to educate employees about their retirement plan, the plan's investment funds and asset allocation strategies. There may be a one-time cost associated with implementing a new plan, as well as ongoing costs for an existing program. Fees may be charged as specific line items or may be part of the service schedule related to investment and/or recordkeeping fees.

EGTRRA
Acronym for the Economic Growth and Tax Relief Reconciliation Act of 2001, which made significant changes in several areas, including income tax rates, estate and gift tax exclusions and retirement and qualified plan rules. In general, the act simplified retirement and qualified plan rules for individual retirement accounts (IRAs), 401(k) plans, 403(b) and pension plans.

Elective deferral
Payroll reduction contributions made by an employer on behalf of an employee pursuant to an election by the employee to have such a contribution made in lieu of cash compensation, which is otherwise payable to the employee.

Eligible employee
An employee who meets a plan's age and service requirement provisions for participation.

Eligible investment advice arrangement
An arrangement that provides that fees (including any commission or other compensation) a fiduciary advisor receives for investment advice or investment of plan assets either do not vary according to the investment option selected or are based on a computer model under an investment advice program that meets regulatory requirements.

Employee Benefit Security Administration (EBSA)
An agency of the Department of Labor responsible for protecting the integrity of retirement plans, health plans and other employee benefits.

Enrollment expenses
Costs associated with enrolling employees in a retirement plan and providing materials to educate them about the plan. There may be a one-time cost associated with implementing a new plan, as well as ongoing enrollment costs. Fees may be charged as a specific line item or may be part of the service schedule related to investment, conversion and/or recordkeeping fees.

ERISA
Acronym for the Employee Retirement Income Security Act of 1974, a federal law that imposes various requirements on voluntarily established pension, health and other welfare benefit plans in private industry, and establishes standards applicable to certain service providers of such plans in order to provide protection for plan participants.

- **3(16) Plan Fiduciary**. The Plan Fiduciary is named in the plan documents and is responsible for regulatory filings, making disclosures to participants, selection and monitoring of all service providers and any other activities called for in the plan documents. Plan administrators, may use other service providers to carry out any or all of these duties, subject to prudent selection and monitoring. The Plan Fiduciary has responsibility for all aspects of the plan, except where specific relief is granted by regulation or transferred to another fiduciary.
- **3(21) Advising Fiduciary**. An Advising Fiduciary is selected by the Plan Fiduciary as an expert to advise the Plan Fiduciary and/or plan participants concerning

investment decisions. Unlike the Managing Fiduciary, the Advising Fiduciary does not have discretionary authority. When prudently selected and monitored, the Advising Fiduciary shares fiduciary responsibility for plan investment decisions with the Plan Fiduciary or Managing Fiduciary.

- **3(38) Managing Fiduciary**. One or more Managing Fiduciaries are selected by the Plan Fiduciary to manage some or all of plan assets and has discretionary authority to select investments. When prudently selected and monitored, the Managing Fiduciary relieves the Plan Fiduciary of the fiduciary responsibility for management and oversight of plan assets. Managing Fiduciaries may perform a variety of related services as agreed to by the Plan Fiduciary.
- **408(b)(2)**. Responsible plan fiduciaries must ensure that arrangements with their service providers are "reasonable" and that only "reasonable" compensation is paid for services. Fundamental to the ability of fiduciaries to discharge these obligations is obtaining information sufficient to enable them to make informed decisions about an employee benefit plan's services, the costs of such services, and the service providers.

ETFs

An acronym for exchange-traded funds, which are investment portfolios that trade like stocks on an exchange and track an index.

Exclusive benefit rule
The ERISA standard that requires plan fiduciaries to act solely for the benefit of the plan participants.

Expense ratio
The cost of administering and managing investments expressed as a percentage of total assets.

Fidelity bond
A bond designed to protect a retirement plan's participants in the event a fiduciary or other responsible person steals or mishandles plan assets.

Fiduciary (under ERISA)
Any person or party who:

- Exercises any discretionary authority or discretionary control with respect to management of the plan or exercises any authority or control with respect to management or disposition of its assets.
- Renders investment advice for a fee or other compensation, direct or indirect, with respect to any moneys or other property of the plan, or has any authority or responsibility to do so.
- Has any discretionary authority or discretionary responsibility in the administration of the plan.

See page 74 for detailed descriptions of ERISA Section 3(16), 3(21) and 3(38).

Fiduciary insurance
Insurance that protects plan fiduciaries in the event that they are found liable for a breach of fiduciary responsibility.

Finders fee
A commission paid to an intermediary or the facilitator of a transaction. The finder's fee is rewarded because the intermediary discovered the deal and brought it forth to interested parties. Depending on the circumstance, the finder's fee can be paid by either the transaction's buyer or seller.

Forfeiture
The portion of a participant's account balance that is relinquished (the nonvested portion) upon termination of employment.

Form 1099R
A form sent to the recipient of a plan distribution and filed with the IRS to document the distribution amount.

Form 5500
A form that all qualified retirement plans — excluding Simplified Employee Pension (SEP) plans and Savings Incentive Match Plan for Employees (SIMPLE) IRAs — must file annually with the IRS. Fees to prepare Form 5500 are usually included in recordkeeping and administration charges.

Front-end load
Sales charges resulting from the purchase of an investment such as a stock or mutual fund.

General Account

In a general account structure, assets are invested in and owned by the insurance company's general account. This means the entire general account of the insurance company, and effectively the ultimate claims-paying ability of the insurer, supports the stable value guarantees. The assets in a general account are not attributable to any single policyholder or liability, and the Employee Retirement Income Security Act (ERISA) excludes the assets supporting these guaranteed insurance accounts from the definition of plan assets and treatment as plan assets.

Group annuity

A series of pooled investment accounts offered by an insurance company that are unitized into shares in order to be reflected on a daily valued 401(k) recordkeeping system. There are two types of group annuity platforms. The first one invests the pooled accounts exclusively in shares of retail mutual funds. Because these pooled accounts are invested only in shares of a particular mutual fund, the value fluctuation is almost identical to that of the actual fund. The only difference is an asset charge or contract fee imposed in addition to the mutual fund expenses. The second type is a sub-advised arrangement in which the pooled accounts are managed with objectives similar to those of a particular mutual fund or managed portfolio, but are not invested in the actual fund itself. These sub-advised funds may either be exclusive to one particular financial institution or made available to a select number of banks and insurance company platforms.

Guaranteed investment (interest) contract (GIC)
A contract between an insurance company and a corporate profit-sharing or pension plan under which the insurance company guarantees a specific rate of return over the life of the contract.

GUST
Acronym for several pieces of legislation passed since 1994, including the Uruguay Round General Agreement on Tariffs and Trade (GATT), the Uniformed Services Employment and Reemployment Rights Act of 1994 (USERRA), the Small Business Job Protection Act of 1996 (SBJPA), the Taxpayer Relief Act of 1997 and the IRS Restructuring and Reform Act of 1998.

Hardship or in-service distribution
A participant's withdrawal of plan contributions prior to retirement. Financial hardship may be a condition for eligibility for this type of withdrawal, which may or may not be permitted under the terms of the plan. Reasons for hardship withdrawals can include coverage of uninsured medical expenses for the participant, a spouse or eligible dependents; purchase of a primary residence (excluding mortgage payments); payment of post-secondary tuition costs for the participant, a spouse or eligible dependents; payments necessary to avoid foreclosure or eviction from the participant's principal residence; funeral expenses for the employee, a spouse, dependents, or beneficiary of the employee; or certain damage repair expenses for the employee's principal residence. These distributions are taxable as early distributions and are generally subject to a 10% penalty tax if the participant is under 59½.

HCE
Acronym for highly compensated employee, who meets one of the following conditions:

- Owned more than 5% of the employer business at any time during the year or preceding year.
- For the preceding year, received compensation of more than a specified dollar amount that is adjusted annually to reflect increases in the cost of living, and if elected by the employer, was in the top 20% of employees when ranked by compensation.

IAR
Acronym for investment advisory representative, an investment advisory company employee whose main responsibility is to provide investment-related advice. IARs must be registered with state authorities and can provide advice only about topics for which they have passed appropriate examinations.

Indirect compensation
Compensation received from sources other than directly from the plan or plan sponsor, including payments to persons or entities for investment management, recordkeeping, participant communication, and other services to the plan as part of a transaction with the plan. Indirect compensation also includes money or "anything else of value" received in connection with services rendered to the plan or in connection with the service provider's position with the plan.

Individually designed plan
A plan established pursuant to a document that is not a prototype document. (See also prototype documents on page 104.) An individually designed plan document is not preapproved by the IRS. In general, individually designed plan documents are more costly to establish and maintain than prototype documents.

Individually managed account
An investment account managed for a single participant based on individual preferences.

Installation fee
A one-time fee charged by some vendors for initiating a new plan.

Investment advice
Refers to any recommendations regarding an investor's portfolio.

Investment management fee
See management fee on page 98.

Investment manager
Any fiduciary other than a trustee or a named fiduciary who:

- Has the power to manage, acquire or dispose of any asset of the plan.
- Is registered as an investment advisor under the Investment Advisors Act of 1940; is registered as an investment advisor under the laws of the state where the principal office and place of business is located; is a bank; or is an insurance company qualified

to perform services under the laws of more than one state.

- Has acknowledged in writing that he is a fiduciary with respect to the plan.

Investment mapping
The process of keeping plan assets invested while changing service providers. This is typically done by ensuring that investment of plan assets maintains the strategy and objective used by the previous provider. For example, assets invested in large-cap growth stocks would remain invested in that asset class under the new provider.

Investment policy statement
The document that provides guidelines for the plan's investment management. It typically sets forth the plan's investment objectives, investment strategies, policies and investment limits.

Investment transfer expense
Charge associated with a participant changing investments and/or investment allocation.

IRS Form 5500
See Form 5500 on page 92.

Keogh plan
A tax-deferred retirement account for self-employed individuals or employees of unincorporated businesses. It can be established as either a defined contribution or a defined benefit plan. Also known as an H.R. 10 plan.

Key employee
An individual who:

- Is an officer of the company that sponsors the plan and earns income in excess of a specified dollar amount that is adjusted annually to reflect increases in the cost of living.
- Owns more than 5% of the company that sponsors the plan.
- Is a 1% owner of the company that sponsors the plan, with income of more than $150,000.

Life cycle fund
A diversified mutual fund designed to offer an appropriate level of risk during different phases of life. Target-risk and target-date funds are two examples of life cycle funds. A target-risk fund targets a specific risk profile (for example, conservative, moderate or growth), while a target-date fund targets a specific future date and generally becomes more conservative over time until it reaches its final risk profile.

Loan fees
Vendors may charge a fee when a plan loan is originally taken, as well as an ongoing fee for administration.

Longevity risk
The risk that the amount of money a person has saved for retirement might not be enough due to increased life expectancy.

Management fee
Fee charged by an investment manager.

Mapping
See investment mapping on page 97.

Master plan
A retirement plan, sponsored by a financial institution, that has already been examined and approved by the IRS.

Matching contribution
An employer contribution to a participant's employer-sponsored retirement plan. The amount of the contribution is based on the amount of the participant's elective deferral contributions. For example, the plan might specify that it will contribute 50 cents for each dollar of elective deferral contributions under its 401(k) plan. Matching contributions are subject to ACP testing.

Money purchase plan
A defined contribution plan that requires the plan sponsor to make contributions on behalf of each participant based on the plan's formula, which is specified in the plan's document. Contributions must be made to a money purchase pension plan regardless of the profitability of the sponsor.

Mortality risk and administrative expense
A variable annuity fee that covers the cost of returning principal in case the annuitant dies.

MPT
Acronym for modern portfolio theory, pioneered by Harry Markowitz in 1952. MPT asserts that risk-averse investors can construct portfolios to maximize expected return based on a given level of market risk. According to the theory, it's possible to

construct an “efficient frontier” of optimal portfolios offering the maximum possible expected return for a given level of risk. MPT cannot guarantee a profit or protect against loss.

Negative election
See automatic enrollment on pages 79.

New comparability allocation
A type of allocation formula for profit sharing plans that allocates disproportionately greater amounts to a specific group of employees. (Also see profit sharing plan on page 104.) The formula is generally designed to maximize the amounts allocated for HCEs within the contribution nondiscrimination limits established by the IRC.

New comparability profit sharing plan with a safe harbor 401(k)
A plan that combines a new comparability allocation formula with safe harbor 401(k) provisions.

NHCE
Acronym for nonhighly compensated employee, which includes employees who do not meet the criteria for an HCE.

Nondiscrimination testing
Various types of nondiscrimination tests applicable to employer-sponsored, tax-qualified retirement plans under the IRC. The tests are generally designed to prevent HCEs from receiving disproportionately greater benefits than NHCEs. The ADP/ACP nondiscrimination tests are two examples.

Nondiscrimination testing expense
Costs associated with the process of nondiscrimination testing to determine whether the plan is in compliance. These costs are often included in recordkeeping and administration fees.

Nonqualified deferred compensation plan
A written agreement between an employer and employee that gives the employee the employer's unsecured promise to pay some future benefit in exchange for services today. Because it is nonqualified, it does not fall under ERISA, meaning it does not receive favorable tax treatment and can freely discriminate. Most nonqualified deferred compensation plans cover only highly paid executive employees.

Nonqualified plan
A retirement plan that doesn't meet the requirements of the IRC to qualify for tax-favored treatment.

Open architecture
A platform that allows for a myriad of investment choices for a plan to utilize for its participants. Instead of offering a set group of funds to pick from, there are usually thousands to choose from.

Opinion letter
A written statement from the IRS as to the acceptability of a prototype plan document.

Orphan plan
A defined contribution plan for which there is no plan sponsor or other plan fiduciary willing to act with respect to the plan.

Participant
An employee who is eligible to participate in an employer-sponsored retirement plan. An employee who is eligible to elect to have his or her employer make elective deferral contributions to a 401(k) plan — but chooses not to — is still considered a participant.

Passive management
Passive Investment Management strategies attempt to replicate the performance of a predetermined benchmark. This strategy is also known an indexing.

PBGC
Acronym for Pension Benefit Guaranty Corp., which was established by ERISA to ensure that benefits will be payable to participants when due if the sponsor of a defined benefit pension plan is unable to make payments. Companies that sponsor defined benefit plans pay premiums to PBGC based on the number of employees in the plan and the current ratio of assets to liabilities in the plan.

Permitted disparity (integrated) allocation formula
Permitted disparity allocation formula refers to a tax-qualified retirement plan that takes into account either benefits or contributions under Social Security in determining the amount of a participant's benefits under the plan. Social Security benefits are used to integrate defined benefit plans and defined contribution plans. In general, profit sharing integrates with Social Security by allocating to plan participants a greater percentage of their compensation in excess of the

Social Security taxable wage base and a lower percentage of their compensation at or below the Social Security taxable wage base. (Also see profit sharing plan on page 104.)

Plan administrator
The person or firm responsible for the administration of a retirement plan, determination of eligibility for benefits and payment of benefit claims.

Plan document/IRS filing fee
Costs associated with preparing and filing required IRS documentation, including the request for a determination letter.

Plan sponsor
A business or employer organization that sponsors the qualified retirement plan and is ultimately responsible for its administration.

PPA
Acronym for the Pension Protection Act of 2006, legislation that affects qualified retirement plans, plan sponsors and plan participants. It contains extensive new rules governing the implementation of automatic enrollment plans, cash balance and other hybrid plans and combined defined benefit pension/401(k) plans for small employers. The act also includes changes affecting retirement plan contributions and distributions, including liberalization of plan rollover rules and new disclosure and reporting rules for ERISA-covered plans, including fiduciary protection for providing certain investment advisory services to participants.

Profit sharing plan
A defined contribution plan that permits the employer to make discretionary contributions. A participant's retirement benefits are based on his or her account balance, which consists of profit sharing contributions, investment earnings and forfeitures. (Also see age-weighted allocation on page 78, new comparability allocation on page 100, permitted disparity (integrated) allocation formula on page 102 and salary ratio allocation on page 110.) A single plan can contain both a profit sharing and an elective deferral feature.

Prototype documents
Documents that provide standard language for different types of retirement plans that offer flexible options within each plan type. Prototype plan documents are sponsored by financial institutions and adopted by employers to create the plan. There are both standard and nonstandard prototypes. Standardized prototype documents are less flexible than nonstandardized prototype documents. Employers who adopt prototype plans are not required to obtain IRS approval (letter of determination) for their plan documents; however, this is a good practice for nonstandard documents.

Prudent man rule
The fiduciary duty under section 404(a)(1)(B) of ERISA that requires a fiduciary to discharge his or her duties to a plan under the prevailing circumstances with the care, skill, prudence and diligence that a prudent man — acting in a like capacity and familiar with such matters — would use in the conduct of an enterprise of like character and with like aims.

QACA

Acronym for qualified automatic contribution arrangement, a type of automatic enrollment resulting from PPA that qualifies for safe harbor and automatically complies with nondiscrimination testing. A QACA arrangement under PPA regulations:

- Does not automatically enroll current employees who:
  - Were eligible to participate in the plan before the automatic enrollment arrangement became qualified.
  - Had deferral elections (or elections not to defer) in place when the automatic enrollment arrangement became qualified.
- Requires that employees who are eligible to participate in the qualified arrangement receive written notice of their legal rights and obligations within a reasonable time prior to the start of the plan year.
- Provides that employer contributions become 100% vested after an employee has completed no more than two years of service.
- Requires that the plan sponsor make either matching contributions (100% of the first 1% of compensation deferred, plus 50% of the next 5% deferred) or non-elective contributions (at least 3% of compensation to all eligible non-highly compensated employees, whether they make deferrals or not).
- Provides for an automatic contribution percentage of at least a minimum specified percentage that ranges from 3% to 6% (depending on how long contributions have

been made for the employee), but not more than 10%. This provision offers guidelines for the step-up feature, which increases the automatic deferral by 1% per year. (Also see automatic enrollment on pages 79.)

QDIA

Acronym for qualified default investment alternative that provides relief from fiduciary liability with respect to automatic enrollment programs when a QDIA (as defined by the DOL) is selected by the plan. The DOL has approved these four types of investments as QDIAs:

- A product with a mix of investments that takes into account the individual's age or retirement date (e.g., a lifecycle or target-retirement-date fund)
- An investment service that allocates contributions among existing plan options to provide an asset mix that takes into account the individual's age or retirement date (e.g., a professionally managed account)
- A product with a mix of investments that takes into account the characteristics of the group of employees as a whole, rather than each individual (e.g., a balanced fund)
- A capital preservation product for only the first 120 days of participation (e.g., a stable value fund)

QDRO

Acronym for qualified domestic relations order, which is a judgment, decree or order that creates or recognizes an alternate payee's (such as a child or former spouse) right to receive all or a portion of a participant's retirement plan benefits. Fees are associated with a distribution resulting from a QDRO.

QLAC
Acronym for Qualified Longevity Annuity Contract, a deferred annuity funded with an investment from a qualified retirement plan or IRA. The annuity contract is a guarantee of monthly payments until death, and it is shielded from stock market downturns. As long as the annuity complies with IRS requirements, it is exempt from the required minimum distribution (RMD) rules until payouts begin after the specified annuity starting date.

QMAC
Acronym for qualified matching contribution, which employers can make to 401(k) plans to correct failed ACP nondiscrimination tests. Qualified matching contributions satisfy the vesting and distribution requirements.

QNEC
Acronym for qualified nonelective contribution, which employers can make to 401(k) plans to correct failed ADP/ACP nondiscrimination tests.

Qualified plan
A retirement plan that meets the requirements of the IRC to qualify for tax-favored treatment.

Recordkeeping fee
See administration and recordkeeping expenses on page 77.

Registered representative
A person who is employed by a brokerage company registered with the Securities and Exchange Commission (SEC). A registered representative must register with the Financial Industry Regulatory Authority (FINRA), pass a qualifying examination, and be licensed by a state securities regulator. They can act as an account executive for clients trading stocks, bonds, mutual funds and other investment products.

Revenue sharing
An agreement between a mutual fund company and a broker dealer whereby payment is made to the brokerage firm from the mutual fund company's investment advisor's revenues or profits. These payments are in addition to any sales charges, 12b-1 fees, redemption fees and deferred sales charges and do not come from the assets of the fund. Advisors receive no additional compensation as a result of these payments.

RIA
Acronym for registered investment advisor, a person or group that makes investment recommendations or conducts securities analysis in return for a fee and who has sufficient assets to be registered with the SEC.

Risk-adjusted returns
A measure of how much an investment returned in relation to how much risk it took on.

Risk parity
A method of portfolio construction and asset allocation in which each holding provides an equal contribution to the overall portfolio risk.

Rollover
A qualifying distribution from a tax-favored retirement arrangement — a 401(k) plan, 403(b) arrangement, SEP plan, SIMPLE IRA, 457 plan or IRA — that is contributed to another qualified plan. There are two types of rollovers from a qualified plan: direct and indirect.

- With a direct rollover, the distribution is paid directly to the trustee or custodian of the receiving arrangement.
- With an indirect rollover, an individual takes a cash distribution from a qualified plan (less 20% withholding) and contributes it (rolls it over) within 60 days of receiving the arrangement.
- A direct transfer of assets between IRAs may also be referred to as a direct transfer of assets.

Roth 401(k) contributions
See designated Roth contributions under 415 limit, common types of contributions on page 75.

Safe harbor 401(k) plan
A plan that provides many of the features and flexibility of a traditional 401(k) without the administrative concerns of ADP/ACP nondiscrimination testing. However, employers must match 100% of employee elective deferrals up to 3% of the employee's compensation, plus 50% of employee elective deferrals on the next 2%

of the employee's compensation, or make a nonelective contribution on behalf of each eligible employee equal to 3% of such eligible employee's compensation. All safe harbor 401(k) contributions are 100% vested immediately.

Salary ratio allocation
A type of allocation possible within a profit sharing plan, which allocates contributions as a flat percentage of compensation among all eligible employees. (Also see profit sharing plan on page 104.)

Salary reduction agreement
A formal agreement between an employer and employee under which the employee agrees to take a reduction in salary or to forgo a salary increase. In return, the employer agrees to deposit the portion deferred from the employee's salary into a benefit plan, such as a 403(b), 401(k), thrift, or cafeteria plan. The agreement may state a specific dollar amount of salary reduction or a percentage of compensation reduction.

SARSEP plan
Salary Reduction Simplified Employee Pension plan, created as a simple alternative to a 401(k) plan for companies with 25 or fewer employees. Employees eligible to participate in a SARSEP have the opportunity to make elective deferral contributions to their SEP plans. Employers may no longer establish new SARSEPs. Contributions may continue to existing SARSEPs.

Self-directed brokerage fees
Transaction and annual fees related to balances in self-directed brokerage accounts.

SEP plan
Simplified Employee Pension plan, a retirement program that permits an employer to make tax-deductible contributions to IRAs established by eligible employees. SEPs can be sponsored by employers of all sizes. This plan is more popular among small employers because it generally has substantially lower administrative costs.

Separate account
An asset account established by a life insurance company, separate from other life insurance company funds, that offers investment funding options for pension plans.

Share classes
Different types of shares issued by a single fund, often referred to as Class A shares, Class C shares and so on. While each class invests in the same "pool" (or investment portfolio) of securities and has the same investment objectives and policies, share classes offer different shareholder services and/or distribution arrangements, resulting in differing fees, expenses and performance results.

- Class A shares typically impose a front-end sales load and tend to have a lower 12b-1 fee and lower annual expenses than other mutual fund share classes. Some mutual funds reduce the front-end load as the size of an investment increases.
- Class C shares generally have a level load and might include a 12(b)-1 fee, other

annual expenses and either a front- or back-end sales load.

- Class R shares are typically provided exclusively to retirement plans and charges can vary based on the plan's requirements and recordkeeping preferences.
- Class R5 shares are often called institutional shares because they are generally intended for financial institutions purchasing shares for their own or their clients' accounts. Class R5 shares have no frontend sales charge and cannot be purchased by the general public.
- Class R6 shares are generally available only to Qualified Plan investors where plan level or omnibus accounts are held on the books of the fund.
- Class Y shares are a class of mutual fund shares that often have a high minimum investment, such as $500,000 per lot, and the added benefit of waived or limited load charges and fees. Due to the high minimum investment required, Y shares are often accessible only to large institutional investors.

Sharpe ratio
A risk-adjusted measure of performance, calculated using standard deviation and excess return to determine reward per unit of risk.

SIMPLE IRA
Savings Incentive Match Plan for Employees IRA, a retirement program that permits eligible employees to make elective deferral contributions to their IRAs and the sponsoring employer to make mandatory

matching or nonelective contributions. Generally, only employers with 100 or fewer employees, each with at least $5,000 of compensation in the prior calendar year, are eligible to establish SIMPLE IRA plans.

Smart beta
Smart beta defines a set of investment strategies that emphasize the use of alternative index construction rules over traditional market capitalization-based indexes. Smart beta emphasizes capturing investment factors or market inefficiencies in a rules-based, transparent way.

Soft dollars
A means of paying brokerage firms for their services through commission revenue instead of through normal direct payments (hard-dollar fees).

Solo 401(k)
A plan designed for businesses with no employees other than the owners and their spouses. Contributions are established by the plan document and are generally 100% vested immediately.

Sponsor
An employer who establishes and maintains a plan.

Stable value fund
An investment vehicle comprising mostly of wrapped bonds, which can be short or intermediate term with longer maturities than other choices such as money market funds. They are paired (or wrapped) with insurance contracts to guarantee a specific minimum return.

Stable value put-24 months
Requires plans invested in a Stable Value Fund to tender an irrevocable 24-month notice in order to redeem their plan's balance in the Fund, other than those withdrawals made solely to accommodate participant benefit payments, and only applies when book value exceeds market value of the fund and a liquidation is requested.

Standard deviation
A statistical measure of the historical volatility of a mutual fund or portfolio. Measures a fund's range of total returns and identifies the spread of a fund's short-term fluctuations.

Subaccount transfer fee
An expense charged against the fund that, in certain situations, is used to offset some of the administrative expenses of a third-party administrator.

Sub-advised
Arrangement in which pooled accounts are managed with objectives similar to a particular mutual fund or managed portfolio, but not invested in the actual fund itself.

Summary plan description (SPD)
A document containing a comprehensive description of a retirement plan, including the terms and conditions of participation. ERISA requires an SPD be distributed to each plan participant within 90 days of becoming a participant and to each beneficiary receiving benefits within 90 days of first receiving benefits.

Sunset provisions
Provisions of EGTRRA that were originally to "sunset," or be automatically repealed, in 2010. The PPA made the EGTRRA provisions related to retirement plans and IRAs permanent. Among the provisions affected were salary deferral limits, contribution limits and catch-up contributions.

Surrender fee
See termination fee on page 115.

Target benefit plan
A type of money purchase plan in which an employer establishes a "target benefit" for employees based on a formula in the plan document, but each employee's actual benefit is based on the amount in his individual account.

Target date fund
A mutual fund that automatically resets the portfolio's asset mix of stocks, bonds and cash equivalents according to a time horizon that is appropriate for a particular investor.

Termination fee
Costs associated with terminating a relationship with a service provider, permanent termination of a plan or termination of specific plan services. Also called "surrender" or "transfer" charges.

Third party administrator (TPA)
An organization that administers retirement plans for an employer. This organization works with the employer as well as the insurer to communicate information between the two, as well as processing claims and determining eligibility.

Top-heavy test
A nondiscrimination test that generally requires a tax-qualified retirement plan sponsor to make minimum contributions and to establish an accelerated minimum vesting schedule when account balances of key employees are disproportionately greater (60% or more) than account balances of nonkey employees (i.e., when the plan becomes top heavy).

Trustee: individual/employer
One or more individuals who are appointed by the employer to act as trustee under its retirement plan.

Trustee: institutional
The bank or trust company designated to serve as the plan trustee. Typically, this type of trustee serves as the custodian of the plan's assets.

Unbundled services
Plan sponsors provide services through a combination of in-house staff and independent service providers for each critical task. It allows for maximum control and the ability to select from among different service providers, including investment options. This model is most prevalent among larger plans that have adequate resources to manage such a plan. Independent consultants are often hired to help construct and manage unbundled plans.

Upside capture ratio
A statistical measure of an investment manager's overall performance in up markets that is used to evaluate how well the manager performed relative to an index during periods when that index has

risen. The ratio is calculated by dividing the manager's returns by the returns of the index during the up market and multiplying that factor by 100.

Vesting schedule
The schedule that determines the portion of a participant's accrued benefit or account balance to which the participant has a nonforfeitable right after completing a specified number of years of service.

Wrap expense
A fee based on all plan assets and in addition to individual fund-related fees. The wrap expense typically pays for bundling of services related to investing plan assets and may include administrative services such as recordkeeping or the preparation of signature-ready Form 5500s.

These definitions have been provided with permission by Invesco Plan*Forward* Foundations℠

Made in the USA
Monee, IL
04 November 2026

67378673R00075